Walking the Path

– The Cree to the Celtic

Walking the Path

– The Cree to the Celtic

Shirley Laboucane

MOON
BOOKS

Winchester, UK
Washington, USA

First published by Moon Books, 2012
Moon Books is an imprint of John Hunt Publishing Ltd., Laurel House, Station Approach,
Alresford, Hants, SO24 9JH, UK
office1@o-books.net
www.o-books.com

For distributor details and how to order please visit the 'Ordering' section on our website.

Text copyright: Shirley Laboucane 2010

ISBN: 978 1 84694 705 6

A CIP catalogue record for this book is available from the British Library.

Design: Stuart Davies

Printed in the UK by CPI Antony Rowe
Printed in the USA by Offset Paperback Mfrs, Inc

We operate a distinctive and ethical publishing philosophy in all
areas of our business, from our global network of authors to
production and worldwide distribution.

CONTENTS

Chapter Six: The Celtic Year and the Elements

Introduction

For the past ten years, I have worked as a professional psychic reader. During the last year or so, I began to fade out psychic readings and instead incorporate the holding of ceremonies for people in their homes for which I do not charge. Often people hear about others having a ritual for a certain event or holiday and think that they too would like to hold one but don't know how. Preconceived ideas about ritual cause people to think they need to change their religion to participate in one. One of the purposes of this book is to introduce people to the art of performing a ritual, without the commitment to changing one's religion or life.

Many people also believe you have to be a pagan to appreciate and perform ritual, which is untrue. For thousands of years people have been drawn together to dance, make music, pray and feast. These activities are all part of the ceremony. The ceremonies in this book are designed to help you become more attuned to yourself, others and nature. You don't have to be a pagan, you don't have to be a shaman or witch, you can be just you with your imagination and a desire to learn and discover.

Ritual is the process of taking time out from the rush of life to connect with what you consider sacred. Performing ceremony properly means slowing down and being in the moment without thinking about yesterday or worrying about tomorrow.

I am a mixture of different nationalities, cultures and belief systems. I think this is very much reflected in my spirituality. I have a Gypsy background, a Catholic background, and an English background, but I have been mostly affected by my Aboriginal background, because I was raised by my native mother. I am half British and half Cree Indian and although I have taken part in strictly Cree ceremonies, it is not a path that attracts me because I am more than just a Cree and I love all the parts of who I am. I have therefore mixed ceremonies together with Celtic and Gypsy influences.

There is a mixture of rituals in this book, some are very serious and some are fun. There are some that I perform when I am alone and some I do with a group — I love to share and dance with other people. I have a general name for my ceremonies and it is the 'sacred hoop' or 'circle' because we always stand in a ring. These ceremonies can be performed alone or with a larger group. They can be performed solely for specific personal needs or the needs of the world.

All the rituals are based on a calendar of ancient festivals and natural cycles of nature. If you would like to do something different besides *h'orderves* and cocktails at your next party, or if you are a serious witch but would like to see what others have to offer in ideas or suggestions for ceremony, then this book is for you.

This book was written for the beginner, the explorer, the type of person who wants to learn and have fun with people and for the experienced pagan who would like to have some fresh ideas for ritual.

Chapter One

Our Mother's Circle

To our ancestors, all of nature including the land itself had a spirit. For the pagan also, the land, her rocks, trees and animals all have spirit and all are connected. And for you, if you listen to the trees they will share their wisdom with you. If you walk as though the soil is sacred, the spirits of nature will converse with you and show you how to heal.

We walk among our brothers and sisters in nature but we have damaged our bond with them. We must learn to walk in silence, walk in unison with Mother Earth's cycles, listen to her wisdom, and feel her heart beat so ours can beat in unison with hers. With our feet firmly planted on Mother Earth, we need to call out to find our purpose and our place within the web of life. Many souls have walked this earth, the living and the dead stand with reverence for our home. People of earth based religions know and understand this deep wisdom, for the mysteries beckon to us to heed and act with purpose and faith so that we can live a meaningful life.

It is time for us to begin to heal our planet. Every day, little by little with small steps turning into larger ones, we can make a difference to this world. We must believe this, we must strive for this, we must be active in this and we must live it.

As an aboriginal, it was taught to me that Mother Earth is alive and this relationship is reflected in the shapes of our ceremonies. Within the sacred circle we are all one, we are all equal and it is the circle's natural flow to promote unity among us. Within the hoop, there is a place for every creature, within the hoop we become aware of our natural place within the scope of creation and for most it is a humbling experience.

We are not here to dominate nature as Christianity taught us, but to be a part of it, to have a reverence for it, to join creations spirit and soar like the eagle.

Performing ceremonies in a circle brings about a completeness of living; the hoop expresses itself in balance and peace. I see the spirit of Mother Earth in glow of a fire, I hear her voice in the sounds of a stream and I feel her presence in the soothing caress of a morning breeze. She is perfect balance with the masculine and feminine side of creation, and I feel natural and whole in this circle of life. When I smudge, her breath becomes smoky and warm and the spirit of the sage lifts itself to Father Sky, reaching out to the Creator, suggesting to his spirit that his presence is desired within a ritual.

When I hold my smudge bowl I see a circle, when I look at Nokum (I affectionately refer to the full moon as Nokum) I see a circle, when I see pictures of the earth I see a circle, when I watch Grandfather Sun rise in the mornings I see a circle. The hoop is birth, life, death and rebirth, it is the individual journey we all must make and like the salmon that struggles against currents to lay their eggs we must struggle to find enlightenment. This struggle is what drew me to the hoop, for within I can focus my spiritual energies more creatively, and it allows me to express my 'personal' belief in divinity and to express my desire to live in harmony with nature. Within the hoop there is order; there is direction, and the ancient wisdom of our ancestors and Earth Teachers (more about Earth Teachers below).

Look at Stonehenge and see the giants who stand with dignity protecting the sacred hoop of power where Celtic people still worship and pray. It is a place where the dead stand with the living, both still being renewed through ritual and prayer.

Wheel Ceremonies

Performing a wheel ceremony is a way to create a holy space where we can manifest and maintain a healing atmosphere by drawing in positive forces. Our ancestors understood the importance of ceremony and how through ritual the Creator speaks to us.

These are the wheels the Creator gave to me and I would like to share them with you. I hope you take these ceremonies and make them your own, and then allow the Creator of the Universe to take you on a sacred passage where you will find your truth and you will experience healing within all levels of your life.

Earth Wheels are also important and in past times were constructed by laying out stones in a certain pattern. Most would follow the basic design of a center stone surrounded by other stones leading away from the center or encircling it. No one knows for sure what these stone circles were used for, but one thing is clear, they were laid out by people in reverence and a belief that they had the power to change their lives through ritual. For these aren't 'Medicine Wheels' they are 'Earth Wheels' and the purpose of these wheels is to reconnect you with nature and to the circle of life. So in the same way, you can arrange stones in whatever way you desire and because this isn't trying to be a Native American wheel you can be more creative.

It is my belief that objects contain the energy of the place they resided in. When you visit certain places that give you a sense of peace, pick up some stones from there and bring them home. Wash them and place them around your home and use them especially for the making of your Earth Wheels. Some of these stones can also be used in other types of wheel ceremonies.

If you choose to use crystals that you have bought from a store, be sure to cleanse them before using. Do this by smudging them with an herb and leaving them out under the moonlight or sunlight for a couple of hours or overnight.

Earth Teachers and Custodians

Earth Teachers are also important to the hoop. An Earth Teacher is a being who can gift us with help from time to time and willingly shares their wisdom with us. They are the four-legged ones, winged ones, creepers and crawlers, swimmers, tree people, rock and plant people. They are also considered our Ancestors just like our two-legged Ancestors. When we honor our Ancestors we honor ourselves and that is why the center of the Earth Wheel is Self.

There are many teachings about Earth Teachers, some are Teachers over societies, totems and clans, but here in this book we are going to discuss them as our personal guides — personal totems that help us on our journey. Earth Teachers help us when we pray, meditate, drum and dance. By giving us their songs and their movements, they share their beauty with us. When you need spiritual help, they will give you their songs and their dance, to heal you and urge you on towards your destiny. When you feel your Earth Teachers in chanting, dancing and meditating, a transfer of power happens from the Teacher to you.

When you find an Earth Teacher or being of nature that is willing to help you, offer them a gift and make a vow to them. For example, I will make a vow that within my Earth Wheel I will always pray with cedar and smudge with cedar in the east.

Custodians — sometimes referred to as Door Keepers — can teach us lessons that help us on our earthly voyage. A Custodian is an Earth Teacher who we make vows to, who we ask to pray for us, to guide us in our lives. They are beings of nature such as birds, animals or trees. Their presence promises that no negativity can enter a ceremony or interfere with prayers. Be aware that a Custodian can refuse to work with you, we don't question why we just accept their wisdom because they are older and wiser than us, so just leave a gift to them and move on to asking another being to help you. Sometimes a Custodian will give you a song or or perhaps a dream as a sign that they are working with you. If you are attracted to willow trees, you can leave the tree an offering of sage or a crystal and then go home. There watch for signs or feelings in the coming days to see if the tree-being is willing to teach you some wisdom. If you love bears, you can say prayers to the Creator and ask if the spirit of the bear is willing to help you, watch for dreams and signs that the bear has wisdom to give you.

Depending on your chosen Custodian, they can also keep your prayers safe and deliver them to the Great Spirit. In the wheel ceremony, it is important to acknowledge the Custodians in each direction when performing the wheel ritual and it is also important to express gratitude to our Earth Teachers so they can continue to impart their wisdom to us.

Through our ceremonies, Earth Teachers and Custodians, we come to realize our place within the sacred hoop. Everything has a being, everything has mystery, and those mysteries lead us back to the source of all Creation, the Great Spirit.

When you are neglecting yourself, your Earth Teachers and Custodians will send you dreams and signs that you have wandered off your path. The Earth Teachers and Custodians want you to be whole, spirituality, mentally and emotionally. It was these precious Ancestors who gave us the Earth Wheel.

In a ceremony, I use a rattle, bell or hand drum in each direction, but you could use singing bowls, homemade musical instruments or whatever tool appeals to you. The use of instruments in this ritual is similar to the way that bells are rung in a Catholic Mass. Some churches ring bells at important parts of the ceremony to alert the parishioners that something important is happening. In a wheel, we do something similar, we are making ourselves and others aware that honor is being paid to our Earth Teachers.

It is a personal choice who will be your Custodian and Earth Teacher, but I do recommend that you pray and meditate on it. Ask for dreams which will reveal them to you, watch your recurring thoughts and feelings, watch nature and see what kinds of creatures come near to you or what plants you are drawn to. Make sure you feel a sense of peace about your choice then begin to study it and learn from its wisdom and experience. There is a small ritual and I will be explaining later in the book that will help you choose a Custodian and Earth Teacher.

Energies

Within the sacred hoop, there are many revered things such as the cardinal directions, colors, crystals and herbs.

Take some time and really think about what kinds of energy you'd like to work with within your Earth Wheel and what resonates best with you. For example, you could use river stones or crystals. You could even use nuts and cones from nature. You can be totally creative because this is *your* wheel.

I like the traditional design of a wheel but sometimes this can change and my stones can change too. This isn't religion, it's being spiritual and creative and in creativity things can change all the time.

My center stone represents spirit and I use blue crystal quartz, for my surrounding stones I use clear quartz and other crystals and then there are my herbs. Each herb or crystal represents a particular item that I use in my daily life. These are smudging herbs such as sage, tobacco, sweet grass and cedar and my crystals such as rose quartz, turquoise, clear quartz and moonstone. Whether the herbs are being used to smudge with or for spiritual or medicinal reasons, these herbs and crystals are medicine to my body, mind and spirit and I love to take time to connect with their energies.

Please note that the Earth Wheel is always changing and just as with the seasons of Mother Earth, the herbs, crystals and so forth of the wheel can change so as to reflect what you are working with and working on in your life.

Crystals and river stones have been used for hundreds of years for healing, protection and dream recall. They are used in these ways within the ceremonies in this book. I will have a list of meanings later on in the book. The moon phases have their own teachings in the wheel and they are significant in its rituals and teachings. In addition, herbs, resins and oils play important roles within the sacred hoop ceremonies and there will also be a list of some these and their spiritual properties later in the book. Sometimes a tree can be a Teacher within a hoop just as sometimes a rose quartz can be a protector in a certain direction. This is the beauty of the hoop; it is truly the hoop of life and all the elements within it.

Smudging

When preparing for the ritual, first your area needs to be cleansed. If you are outside, remove twigs, rocks, garbage and general debris from the area. If you are inside, clear away all clutter. Smudge the area with one of the sacred herbs such as sage, or if you have moon water or holy water sprinkle your area with it. We do this so there will be no negative energies interfering with our intentions and prayers. Next smudge yourself — and other people if you are not alone — than take a feather or using your hand wave smoke from the smudge pot to the seven directions as follows. Fan your smoke upwards to the Creator or God and Goddess, then fan smoke to the ground to Mother Earth, then fan smoke to your chest for Spirit, then fan the smoke to the East, South, West and North, and then back to the East where you started. In each direction, say a prayer.

Let's discuss smudging in more detail. First fire is involved here so it is better not to have any small children around. There will be smoke so make sure there is some ventilation, be sure no small embers drop on anything, and last but not least be sensible and careful.

Smudging is the process of burning herbs, oils and resins to cleanse negative influences from the body, an object or a given area.

Some people remove jewelry for the smudging. I don't

because I want my jewelry to be cleansed as well, I do though remove my glasses for it.

Before you begin smudging yourself, clear your mind and untangle your thoughts. Breathe in and out a few times to allow yourself to be centered for your ceremony, focus on the ritual you are about to do, which is the smudging or clearing of your energy field. This is a ceremony all of its own, it is a sacred act. Take a few minutes to say a prayer of thanks and ask the herb for cleansing your energy and to give you strength and protection during the ritual. Whatever herbs you have to hand whether sage, sweet grass, cedar, rosemary or another preference, let your spirit guide you to what herbs are best for the ritual. Put the herbs in a fireproof container such as an abalone shell. You can also use a ceramic container with sand in the base. On top of this put burning charcoal (this is special charcoal for incense burning available in New Age stores); place your herbs on top. The materials do get hot so be careful.

You can draw on or just pay homage to the elements while smudging. The shell is water, the matches produce the fire, the rising smoke is air and the herb is earth.

Invoke the power of love while you smudge. Starting with your hands, wash them in the smoke and using your hand or feather, fan the smoke from the bowl moving down to your feet. Next fan the smoke around your lower legs and slowly bring it up to your chest area. Place the bowl on a table or hold it if you must and fan smoke over your head. Lastly, cup some smoke and hold it to your heart for a few seconds and give a small prayer of thanks.

You can do a fireless smudge by gathering some herbs in a bundle and sweeping them all around your body to cleanse it. Some people prefer essential oils and will either dip some herbs in oil, or will use an oil burner and allow the scent of the oil to cleanse their aura. I have done this with an oil burner and when I can smell the oil being released, I cup my hands over it and fan myself with the scent of the essential oil, it works nicely. Another avenue you can try is resins. Using a fireproof container and some sand and charcoal put a small chuck of resin on the burning charcoal and when it starts to smoke, fan the resin smoke over your body saying prayers.

When smudging an area, take your smudge pot and walk clockwise in a circle. When you have finished stand in the center of your area and offer smoke to the seven sacred directions of the wheel as follows:

Fan smoke upwards to the Creator, fan smoke downwards to Mother Earth, fan smoke to your heart for sacred self, fan smoke to the east, then south, west and north and move on again towards the east. Give thanks for this blessed space.

After I have smudged — and right before a ritual — I like to perform a physical demonstration of the sacred directions. I center myself for a second and with a deep cleansing breath, I bring my hands to my chest in a position of prayer. Next, I bring my hands over my head towards Father Sky. Dropping my left hand so that it is outstretched, I affirm the Custodians of the Hoop. I follow this with lowering my right hand until it is outstretched at my side and then I affirm the Earth Teachers. Lastly, I swoop my hands downward and bring them together again to point downwards and affirm Mother Earth. Lastly, I bring my hands back to where they started in a prayer position at my chest and affirm my sacred self.

Chapter Two

The Stones of the Earth Wheel and the Ceremony

Each stone within the sacred hoop means something, and the meaning of the stones should mean something special to you. My hope is that you will meditate on the wheel and ask for the meanings of the stones to be revealed to you. Meantime, I would like to make some suggestions by sharing the meanings of my own stones to help you on your journey into the hoop.

Be mindful that performing a wheel ceremony can bring about miracles, so give it the respect it deserves. Whenever I perform a wheel ceremony there is a fire that burns on the astral plane, I see this clairvoyantly. I have meditated to see if I can find out why this fire burns and I believe the fire is a beacon for attracting beings of light, for sometimes I see Indians in spirit gathered around it.

Depending on what kind of ceremony I am doing, the center stone can mean the Creator, the God and Goddess, the Great Mystery, Spirit or the Sacred Fire. Let us say that the center stone means God and Goddess, and in my wheel, the surrounding seven stones stand for Mind, Body, Spirit, Fire, Water, Earth and Air. It is your Earth Wheel so you can make it how you want. It is up to you how many stones you want to use and how you want to arrange them. You may even want to decorate it or perhaps paint the stones; this is particularly affective if you are working indoors.

To begin the ritual place on your altar smudging supplies, candles, all the elements displayed and a bell or shaker. If you are having the ceremony outdoors with a bonfire, before you create the fire offer some herbs to the ground, say a prayer for good feelings during the ritual and then take a broom if you use one and ceremonially sweep the area (I smudge myself, the area where I will do my ceremony).

Next, take a branch from an evergreen tree and sweep the area invoking the power of the Creator to bless and heal all who enter the circle. You can choose colored ribbons that are sacred to you (colors meanings can be found at the end of the book) and attach these ribbons to the sticks that are used to start your fire. It's vital to remember to be in a state of joy, and to revere and respect all the items that are being used in this ceremony, for even the matches are important.

The stones that are leading away from the center stone appear as spokes in a wheel. Whether inside or outside, if you are making an altar of an Earth Wheel, it's important that the stones and all items are smudged and given thanks for. Think of who/what these stones will represent in your ritual. For example, I will take a crystal and while holding it will think of sage and the scent of this herb and how it makes me feel when I use it. I will also consider its magical properties and how I can use this herb to assist me on my path. I will say a prayer to it asking it to bless my stone and always to be present in my wheel. I then ask the herb to infuse the stone with the intentions of health and protection. Another idea is to have images of your herbs painted on your stones or perhaps carve the stones into lanterns.

First Quadrant — East — Fire

The Eastern direction for me is fire, it is morning, and it is spring. The color that resonates for me with this direction is yellow and there is a reason this is so. Our world is filled with color and color can have a powerful effect on humans. We have colors that remind of us of holidays, funerals and such. Color is an energy and so color helps us transmit our prayers more effectively. The colors you choose must resonate with you and so focusing on the color can give your prayers power.

Three stones lead us to the Cardinal Stone. Each of these stones represents an herb, resin or crystal such as tobacco, frankincense and fire agate. The Cardinal Stone is the last stone in the line farthest from the center that faces east and for myself I like to have a tree there such as the Cedar Tree. Cedar teaches me to accept the blessings and gifts given and always give thanks for them. Cedar reminds me to be silent and to have the patience that the Creator does hear my needs.

In each of the four quadrants, there are three moons. A creature is associated with each moon, and focusing on the eastern part of the wheel, the creatures that resonate with the moons are birds. As the moons are spring moons, I may have as the March moon Eagle, the April moon Chickadee and the May moon Robin. Each of these birds will have a message attached to it. For instance, May is Robin's moon because of the red breast and the Creator shows me that he gives me the courage to face my fears and to conquer them. Moon meanings are important and this is just to give you ideas of what I do. There are times when my moons might be a rose moon because I am praying a lot to Mother Mary and I might want to connect with her. This isn't a religion and it isn't suppose to lock you into always praying to these creatures, so be creative and free with it and enjoy the rituals.

This part of my wheel is about my spirituality and the element of fire. It indicates new beginnings, new opportunities, new journeys, prosperity and growth, which means this is the gate through which renewal comes into my life. Affirmations that relate to this subject should be proclaimed here and offerings made to the Universe. My spirituality is also here and this is the direction I face when praying about my spiritual needs and my psychic development.

Second Quadrant — South — Water
The Southern direction for me is water, it is afternoon, and it is

summer. My sacred color here is blue. In the southern direction I have three stones leading to the Cardinal Stone which are sweet grass, lavender, and lavender essential oil. These herbs and oils are associated with calming and helping with emotional balance because in this southern direction I like to pray for my emotional needs.

These stones lead me to the Cardinal Stone, which represents Apple Tree. Apple Tree reminds me that only the Creator knows how many apples are in an apple seed in other words I try not to over analyze things in my life but leave those mysteries to the greatest mystery of all, the creator of life.

The moons in this part of the wheel are summer moons, a time to meditate on warmth, life, relaxation, and a slowing down to savor life and love. They are the fellowship of the swimmers so here I have Orca Moon who teaches me about family and responsibility, Dolphin Moon reminds me to take time to enjoy the journey. The last moon in this slice of the wheel is Trout Moon and the teachings around Trout are about abundance and storing up for tougher times.

Third Quadrant — West— Earth

The Western direction for me is Earth and it is evening. My sacred color is red and here the moons are autumn. My Earth Teachers of the stones are cedar, which I will burn in this direction, and Tiger's Eye and Myrrh. I am attracted to these items because they relate to physical things in my life, for example Tiger's Eye is a crystal that I have used in exams and legal situations, cedar has been used for sprains. Myrrh makes me think of male energy and when I burn it I feel grounded and assertive. The earth stones lead to the Cardinal Stone that represents the Willow Tree who teaches me to trust my intuition.

The moons are the fellowship of the creepers and crawlers. Full moons are autumn time and it reminds me to get out and enjoy the beauty of the season and to appreciate the harvests in my life. Meditate on your moon meanings in this direction. Before each ceremony, always ask what the teaching is for this direction. Write it down and read over it or share it with a group.

Fourth Quadrant — North — Air

The Northern direction for me is Air and it is night. My sacred color is white and it is winter. Three Earth Teacher stones represent items that help me mentally because this is the direction of my mental health. The three items here that help is sage, which I sometimes offer here, Rose essential oil because it helps me feel clear-headed and Turquoise, which I love to meditate with when I am seeking answers. These items lead to the Cardinal Stone, which is Pine Tree who teaches me that life is eternal and that I am part of the circle of life.

Here the moons represent animals and so it is the fellowship of the four legged. The winter moons are Buffalo who teaches me to chose my words carefully and think before I speak, Wolf reminds me that I must plan wisely and Raccoon teaches me to look before I leap. The moons here teach me that the winter is a time to conserve my strength, monitor my progress in achieving my plans. Winter moons are resting time moons, taking time with family and friends and the gift of giving. These can be the base of your moon teachings during this time.

The Directions of the Hoop

First Direction

The First Direction of the Pagan Wheel is Upward, it is the entrance of the Sacred Hoop and the path way set before the Traveler.

With a whisper, He or She sings our name. We realize we are never alone — we are never powerless. Here within the Sacred Hoop we can accept ourselves for who we are, from this place we can rest and begin a journey that will guide us to embrace our inner wisdom. This is a journey of self-discovery but it is also a journey of self-healing and healing our planet, communities and families.

My sacred color here is blue. The color in the first direction is special, as it has to be a color that resonates with your belief in the divine. I look up, face the sky shake my rattle, and give thanks to the Creator.

Imagine the Creator's hand caressing your face. Taking my tobacco in my left hand, I bring it to my heart. I place my prayers into the herb.

Looking upward, I affirm to the Creator of all living beings to hear my prayers of gratitude and accept my offer of tobacco. I then offer my tobacco to my smudge bowl and as I watch the smoke ascend upwards, I know my prayers ascend with the smoke. I then like to chant, if I am alone I just dance around with my drum in a circle. If I am with a group we do this all together just as if I am in a group everyone offers tobacco together.

Second Direction

The Second Direction of the Wheel is Downward and Mother Earth. Our mother creates a web out of the memories of our Ancestors. Fragile, tangible these strands are not easily broken for they hold the mysteries of humanity. She shares her esoteric wisdom only with those who will listen. She waits for us to acknowledge her power as the Eternal Mother, who loves us, who sustains our lives, who holds our secrets. Mother Earth desires to teach us to be gentle on ourselves, to remember our lives are fleeting, yet we are eternally connected to her and all of nature. She desires us to nourish the best that is within each of us.

We are relatives to everything on this planet; here we honor the invisible connection between us all. This is the teaching of this direction.

I look down to Mother Earth my foundation and I offer a

sacred herb of sweet pine. I acknowledge my sacred color, which is green. I shake my rattle I hold my herb in my left hand and bring it to my heart. I whisper my prayers into the herb and then offer it to the smudge bowl or fire, I then chant and dance.

Third Direction

The Third Direction is the Center of the Wheel, our oneness, the one in all, a place of perfect balance — our spirit.

The color here is purple. Here, I offer lavender to my smudge bowl or fire. I shake my rattle, pick up my herb with my left hand, and bring it to my heart. I then picture my prayers being infused into the herb. I whisper my needs and then release them to the fire and chant and dance.

Fourth Direction

In the Fourth Direction, we look to the East. Out of the blackness of night arises the sun. The sun streams across our faces, its warmth stirs within us with a fervor for life. All children need warmth and security, our Grandfather sun gives us his warmth freely without asking anything in return.

Just as our Creator loves us and gives us all we need, in this direction we are shown that we cannot seek prosperity and achievement for ourselves and forget about the state of our communities and families. Our ambitions must include the needs of others.

The color here is yellow. In this direction I offer juniper, I turn to face east and I shake my rattle. With juniper in my left hand, I bring my hand to my heart and place my feelings and requests into this sacred plant then offer the herb to my smudge bowl. I finish this direction chanting an elemental song and dancing.

Fifth Direction

In the Fifth Direction, I look South just as my Ancestors looked up into the night sky and gaze at the splendor of the universe and the moon, her iridescence lights up the hillsides, her moonbeams licking at the shadows of night. Memories stand in the darkness calling to us, whispering to us not to forget who we are, where we came from, pacts made, promises broken. Look to the past to understand the present.

For thousands of years our Ancestors gathered by the light of the moon, hoping to learn from her wisdom. Grandmother asks us to remember our pasts to meditate on lessons learned and lessons failed, and to use that knowledge wisely. Honor the sufferings of our Ancestors remember their pain but also draw strength from their joy and love.

The color here is dark blue it represents the sacrifices that our loved ones made and to honor their spirits. In this direction I offer sweet grass, I turn and face the south and shake my rattle, I take my herb into my left hand and bring it to my heart, I place my prayers inside this herb and then I offer it to the smudge bowl or fire. Chanting and singing follow.

Sixth Direction

In the Sixth Direction, I look West. I affirm that as a granddaughter of the God and Goddess I am strong, and confident of who I am my sacred color here is red the color of our lifeblood. Here the medicine I offer is cedar. To some the cedar is the tree of life to me she is one of the grandmothers of our land. I turn west and shake my rattle. I take the cedar into my left hand and make my prayers then I offer the cedar to the smudge bowl or fire. I ask the Door Keepers watch over my prayers to the Creator. I chant and sing.

Seventh Direction

Our final destination in the Earth Wheel is the Seventh Direction and to the North. Here is the color white, which stands for prosperity, growth, and home. I turn to the north and shake my rattle. I offer sage here, I pick up my sweet pine with my left hand bring my hand to my heart and say my prayers. I know that as the smoke raises so do my prayers to the Creator and to Goddess.

After this final direction, I chant and dance for a bit then I sit or stand for a few moments honoring all the elements involved in my ritual and giving thanks for everything.

After a ritual, I like to select a card from the earth ceremonies oracle deck and meditate upon it. Then I take up my rattle or drum and make some soft music.

If there is a group, some might want to form a circle and dance slowly around the fire thinking of the bond between you all now because you have shared this sacred observance. The prayers have been sent, you have honored your ancestors you have given thanks and made your requests known to the Great Mystery and your journey has begun.

Note: if you are performing an Earth Wheel ceremony with a group of people, make an entrance to the wheel in the eastern direction. Mark off that gate by placing a torch or candles on either side so that the people will pass through the fire and therefore be cleansed.

During the ceremony itself, it would be ecologically mindful if candles were placed into natural items such as glass, earthenware, gourds, pumpkins and so forth. If you're talented enough you could carve totem animals/creatures into your pumpkins or paint them onto glass jars. During the summer months, when pumpkins aren't around use your imagination and use watermelon, cantaloupe, honey melons. All natural candles are best.

The Earth Wheel ceremony isn't a Native American ritual or a Celtic ritual; it is a ritual that celebrates nature and our place in it. There is no right or wrong way to perform this, remember this isn't religion, it is being ecologically aware of our natural environment and connecting to it physically, emotionally and spirituality.

Chapter Three

The Earth and Sky Rituals

Mother Earth, she remembers everything, she is aware of everything that goes on, she sustains our lives, she feeds us, and this is our home. Take time to slow down and restore that connection to earth. Break free from routine and walk to where the cedars stand and absorb their wisdom and patience. Breathe in the scent of the trees and soil and get your hands in the dirt as you gather fallen boughs.

Kiss a crystal or stone that you leave as a gift and ask the cedar to pray for you, they will you know, they will remember your kindness and they will remember your tears. There is nothing more loving than Grandmother Cedar. Stand in awe of the sunset and gather your thoughts or let them drift away. Have a bonfire or a smudge pot and allow the smoke to drift upwards and be a part of Mother Earth's fragrance, your prayers carried to the four corners by the sacred smoke. Expect answers to prayers give thanks, feel your feet in the soft earth, feel your connection to your mother. Watch as Grandfather Sun sinks into the darkness and *feel* the darkness of Mother Earth, her darkness reminds me of my mother's black eyes … soft and wise.

Sunset Earth Wheel Ceremony
(Feeding Mother Earth)

Dusk before you pass into night bathe my spirit as the water bathes the shore

Sunsets are so spectacular they make us want to honor them in some special way. Dusk is the time of day when the light is mysterious and enchanting. Our ancestors believed that the veil between the living and the dead was thin during this brief time of day.

It also marks the end of our day, a time when we want to unwind and reflect on what has gone on in our day and what tomorrow will be like. A sunset ritual is for giving thanks and it is for cleansing our energies of 'stuff' from our day and to welcome the night ahead.

First start with smudging your area then yourself and offer smudge smoke to the seven directions.

Facing west allow the smoke from your smudge bowl to drift upwards into the air say your prayers of thanksgiving for your day and thank Mother Earth for your life, your home, your loved ones and so on.

My sacred color here is red because red is the color I see in the sunset and red is the color of my lifeblood ... that blood nourishes my body. Here also is the element of earth, which means stability, balance, moderation and home.

Take your rattle or drum and then rotate around until you are facing west again and pray:

Four winds, messengers of the Creator take my prayers west to where Grandfather Sun rests and gives way to darkness. Hear my prayers.

I give thanks to the Great Spirit for this day. I give thanks Mother Earth for my food, my home, and my loved ones. Talk to me Great Spirit in my dreams show me the beauty and gentleness in all things. Mother Earth, you are my mother, you sustain my life and without you, I would not exist. Your medicines heal me, your foods sustain me and your beauty teaches me truth, honor and respect. You give so much and I want to give something back to you in thanksgiving, please accept my gift that I offer this evening.

Then take something special like bannock, berries or a bit of salmon and offer it to the earth, to a stream or to a fire.

If you are offering a wreath of cedar, do this with much reverence, for this tree is extremely sacred and this plant is aware of its power. Tie your ribbons lovingly onto it and think of the God and Goddess or the Great Spirit. Feel this tree, smell its fragrance, it has offered itself up for you to heal you, to connect you. Only take limbs that are on the ground and leave some tobacco or something else such as a crystal as an offering. Hold your cedar and chant or sing, feel its vibration ask the tree to speak to the Great Spirit and thank her for all her blessings. When you offer the branch do so with care place it on the ground where no one can disturb it, offer it to water, string it in a tree, or burn it when the smoke rises be meditative that the tree is assisting your prayers.

Note: If you are having a group of people over and would like to make your ritual a little more elaborate, then you might want to consider incorporating a Cedar Ceremony into it.

Prepare boughs of cedar with strips of ribbon of the sacred colors. Have enough boughs for everyone, there can be several boughs of the same color. The purpose is that each person selects a bough and explains what the color means to them and how they notice the color in nature. Allow each person to say a prayer of thanks to Mother Earth then offer the bough to a fire or place on an altar. If you are placing the bough on an altar after the ceremony those boughs must be offered in some fashion to the earth.

There can be variations to this ritual. I realize that not all people live in places where they can offer food to the outdoors, so it is fine to offer the smoke from herbs instead of food.

Sunrise Ritual Prayer
The Creator is the Great Mystery, the Great Spirit that is in all and connects us all, and the Divine Intelligence.

The gifts from creation are pure and perfect for us. When our circle is out of balance, his strength can heal us and lift us to a higher state of perfect peace.

When you perform this tobacco ceremony at sunrise, pray with your whole being, be grateful for the sky, the sun, the moon and earth, we are relatives to everything in nature. We are born, we live, die and are reborn; our lives are a true circle in motion, let our circle be filled with kindness let us walk in love and be aware of the sacred in all things.

The spirit of the eagle is within us when we pray to the Creator.

Sunrise Prayer

Hear my prayers four quarters of the earth, give me the strength to walk in wisdom and respect for all my relatives the two legged, four legged the swimmers, the creepers, the crawlers and the winged ones. When I breathe let me inhale the ancient air of my ancestors whose voices I hear in the winds, I am grateful to the Creator for his messengers the four winds of the four kingdoms.

I come before you as one of your children I am weak, I need your strength, I am afraid I need your shield, I am lost I need your light. Make me ready Creator to come to you, each day let me be mindful that life is precious and we are here to live a life that is charitable. Teach me your ways. Teach me the path of beauty and truth.

Sunrise Earth Wheel Ceremony
The World is Within Me

Three things cannot be long hidden: the sun, the moon, and the truth.
~Buddha

This ceremony is to be done at sunrise and outside if you can. If you need to work indoors, make sure you face the east. This is a powerful ritual and is also a healing ritual. If you are sick or have someone in your life that is sick, bring friends together and perform this ceremony for healing.

The sacred offering for this ritual is tobacco, the Earth Teacher for this ceremony is the eagle and we are praying to the Creator. The spirit of the eagle is within us when we pray to the Creator.

Hold the tobacco and make a connection with it. The tobacco shouts your prayers to the Creator, this plant knows it is powerful, and this plant is a powerful friend to have when pleading for help.

Find a spot where you will be able to view the sunrise and find somewhere private. If indoors try to do this at a window facing east, it is important to see the sunrise. Smudge yourself, the area and offer smudge smoke to the seven directions, perform your physical demonstration of the sacred directions. Using herbs move sunwise (clockwise) and sprinkle the area with tobacco (if indoors you don't have to sprinkle the floor with tobacco but if you do after the ritual sweep it up and deposit it outdoors.

Set up your altar and bring to it your smudge bowl, pipe, offering of food/herbs, hand drum, rattle, blanket, and tobacco and pipe mixture. Lay all your items on your ceremonial blanket. Sit yourself on a pillow and take some deep breaths, relax, focus on this task and nothing else, let your worries and cares fall away from you.

Time stands still in a ritual and this is a very special time that you are making for yourself and the Creator. Then visualize a beautiful circle of light encircling yourself and the area this is your protection.

Center yourself in the moment and take your drum or rattle and make some music, soft music so as not to break this moment of tenderness with yourself and your Creator. Say the prayer to the Creator as in the sunset ceremony above.

With your left hand take some tobacco and offer it to the smudge bowl giving thanks to Mother Earth for the tobacco. Now light your tobacco, as you watch the smoke rise upwards ask Earth Teacher eagle to take your prayers to the Creator and to Earth Mother. This is the time to ask for a miracle in your life, make your requests now.

After prayers are said, take up your drum or rattle and make some soft music and meditate on your prayers.

Now take your bowl of herbs or food (this can be bannock, salmon, herbs, flowers, feather or leaves from a tree or something else from nature and sprinkle it with tobacco. Raise it up and thank the Creator for all that is coming into your life. Affirm the abundance that is now in your life. Pray for our Mother Earth and all of her creatures and all of humanity.

Drum softly, relax feel the warmth of the sun, be in a state of faith and assurance that all is well.

The next part of this ritual is optional if you like pick up your ceremonial pipe and add your smoking mixture to it. Watch the smoke spiral upwards to the Creator, remember all your Ancestors, and give thanks to the spirits that are with you every day helping you and guiding you. These beings are a gift from the Creator, remember to again give thanks for their help, miracles are coming to you and the answers to the questions that you have asked are coming to you, ask for signs, dreams and so forth to come into your life.

Sit now and drum again for a bit watching the sun come up, feeling your connection to all living things, being grateful for this day. When you stand, bow to Grandfather Sun thank him for his warmth and the life giving energy he sends to you and to Mother Earth. Take your time to clear your space doing it with reference if you did this ritual indoors take your herbs outside and offer it to the earth then come in and clear your space.

Heaven cannot but be high. Earth cannot but be broad. The sun and moon cannot but revolve. All creation cannot but flourish. To do so is their TAO. But it is not from extensive study that this may be known, nor by dialectical skill that his may be made clear. The true sage will have none of these.

~Chuang Tzu

Ceremonial foods you can offer are corn, wild rice, beans, maple sugar, bannock, berries, salmon or some kind of fish, pumpkin, squash, game meat, honey, wheat, oats and mead. Draw from your ancestry for your sacred foods.

Note: Ceremonial foods aren't to be eaten in this ritual, offer the food to a river, burn them in a fire, or place them by a tree.

Chapter Four

A Collection of Mixed of Rituals

Smudging Ritual

Smudging is a way of clearing items, places and people of any negative energy. Place your herbs into a smudge bowl give a quick prayer of thanks to the Creator for your smudge pot and then place the herbs and/or resins you will be using within your smudging container. Light the herbs and taking a feather and in a sunwise fashion, walk around the room using your feather to fan the smoke. Earth the room asking for it to be cleansed and cleared of all negative influences.

For smudging objects, fan the smoke with a feather around the item asking that all negative energies be removed from it.

When smudging a person start a few feet from their body and move in a sunwise way around their body fanning the smoke towards them. Keep rotating around them until you are closer to their body. Smoke around the feet upwards to the head all the while moving in a circular fashion. Pay more attention to areas that you feel are blocked or have sickness. When you feel the entire body has been smudged with the smoke, ask the person to cup the smoke into their hands and bring it to their heart in a ceremonial gesture of bringing the peace of the herb into their emotional well-being.

When I am offering smudge smoke to the seven directions, I start with fanning the smoke in an upwards gesture to the Creator or the Divine Love. I always ask for blessings and protection from this universal source of all life and love. I then offer smoke to Mother Earth and give thanks for all my food, medicines and home. The smoke is then fanned to my heart area and I bless myself, bless my past, present and future. This is followed by offering smoke to the east and asking the winds of the east to carry my prayers to the Creator. I then ask the eastern winds to bring me my messages from the Divine that will improve my life. I then repeat in all the directions. When I have gone full circle, I hold still for a moment and then the area is blessed and I am blessed.

Birthday Ritual

When holding a birthday ritual I like to incorporate the smudging ritual before the ceremony.

After smudging is done for each person, then we proceed to the next part of the ritual. Let us say for instance that you are having this ceremony in your living room. Then make sure the room is tidy then smudge the room. Have two tables or two candles that will act as gates that everyone must pass through to go into the living room where the ceremony will take place. On those tables, you can have some holy water, blessed statues, angels, cleansing crystals, protective herbs such as tobacco or sage, the choice is yours. The purpose of the blessed tables or candles is to not let any negativity in. People can carry unwanted energies with them and are not aware of it. The blessed entrance is set up to keep those energies out. After everyone is smudged and walks through the blessed gates, they can stand in a circle. Now you can take a wand, prayer stick, broom or simple a branch from a tree and perform the next act.

Take your wand, prayer stick or broom and point it in the east and begin to turn clockwise and pray:

In the east, south, west and north
A perfect circle casts love and hope
A perfect circle casts out fear and pain
We gather here tonight to raise the vibration of positivity and power
Come all; you are invited to this sacred space.

We have come here to celebrate ..... (whatever ceremony it is)

Then everyone holds their broom or each other's hands and walk three times sunwise in a circle this signifies turning of the yearly wheel.

Suggested chant: Spiral Chant or Cherokee Morning Chant (which can be found at the end of the book).

Stop, while the Circle Keeper says a prayer.

We ask for the God and Goddess's blessings over this gathering

(Face east): *Great Spirit of Light place of the rising sun Let there be light on our paths, let our fire always burn brightly with love and compassion. We thank you for the gift of fire.*

(Face south): *Great Spirit of Love; fill our cups with your sacred waters. We thank you for water, it is the lifeblood of Mother Earth and it sustains our lives and all life on this planet. We thank you for the gift of water.*

(Face west): *Great Spirit of Life; thank you for our bodies thank you for our paths, never let us forget our connection to Mother Earth and our connection to spirit. Thank you for the gift of earth.*

(Face north): *Thank you Great Spirit for the Creation of the universe and souls. Thank you for the air we breathe, thank you for the winds of creation — the four winds from the four kingdoms. Thank you for the messages they bring to us. We thank you for the gift of air.*

May the gifts of nature and blessings of the wise sustain us this night and throughout our lives.

The above is a casting of protection and if you are alone subside we/our — for me/my.

On your center table, you will have three candles and while everyone is gathered, you will pray over them and light them for the birthday person. The first candle represents mind, the second represents body and the third candle represents soul.

Light the first candle and say a prayer for the person that they will have peace of mind in the coming year. Next light the second candle and say a prayer that they will have excellent health now and in the future. Finally, as you light the third candle ask that they will have safe passage on their spiritual journeys and discoveries. You can make your prayers more personal and longer to suit the person's personality.

Then everyone should offer an herb or resin to the smudge bowl, with the left hand hold your herb to your heart and place prayers for your friend into those herbs and ask the herbs to pray for this person to have a blessed day and a blessed year to come. Next burn your herbs and as the smoke lifts into the air so do your prayers to the Creator. You finish with some chanting, singing and drumming. Perhaps Spiral Chant and Mother Earth Chant (which can be found at the end of the book).

In closing, the ceremony let everyone sing happy birthday and then the Circle Keeper leads everyone out of the space.

Tipi Ceremony

Let me say that not everyone can make a tipi or has the space to have one. I don't have one, I don't have the backyard for a tipi but I do remember my mother talking about them. She was a Cree Indian from Alberta. A Plains Cree, she is the one who took me to the Sundances and taught me how to pray as an Indian. If you are like me and you don't have a tipi you can bless your home, instead of your tent or tipi if you choose.

When natives make something, there is always a purpose and a meaning to it. The tipi structure is referred to as a woman, my mother talked about how the tipi was a grandmother's skirt and everyone could find shelter under her cloak. Therefore, the tipi is a female symbol and the spirit of women is in this tipi. Men can help build a tipi but women should be present and a woman needs to bless the ground before they begin. It is a woman who walks around the tipi once it's up and conducts the prayers, and it is a woman who cures it with smoke. During the feast, it is the women who give their teachings for the poles.

When you make a tipi the first time it goes up it needs to face the east. We face the door east because this direction means the beginning of Creation.

Before you begin, you should offer tobacco and give thanks to the Creator. Hold your tobacco in your left hand and connect with how sacred this herb is and what it can teach you. In other words, link with the plant, then bring it to your heart, and infuse your prayers into the herb. Sprinkle it around the area you wish to place your tipi.

The tipi is a woman she brings her children in from the cold and gives them shelter. Every pole has a teaching and some tipis have fifteen poles. Before you make your tipi look to your spiritual walk, ask yourself what lessons are important to you, what have you learned and what your personal ethics are. Place these beliefs into your poles, again offer tobacco and pray that the woman spirit of your tipi will embrace these teachings. The beliefs you place into your poles should be written down so you can refer back to them in a future ceremony. They must be beliefs that benefit the family or community because a tipi's spirit is one of community. Make sure your teachings are written down in love and in beauty. Each pole needs the other to make the balance, so each teaching needs to support the other and those teachings must support the family. Look up at the poles, we all come together to share in the Creator, no matter what our paths are we come from the same Great Mystery, the source of all creation. The rope that binds the poles together are our sacred teachings that each of us carry with us in life and we are all threaded together in this circle of life.

When you have finished making your tipi, you can encircle it or walk clockwise around it offering tobacco and praying. Then build a bed of charcoals or something to burn herbs on, make sure there is some ventilation. When the heat is ready place herbs on the coals, you could use sweet grass, cedar, juniper or sage. Once the smoke has got going leave the tipi and allow the smoke to 'cure' your tipi. While you are outside of your tipi, do some drumming or chanting until the smoke dies down. Then when you are ready, go in, remove your herbs, and place them by a tree. Give thanks to those herbs for blessing your tipi. Decorate the tipi with symbols that are sacred to you. After all the prayers and blessings, have a feast for friends and family in your tipi and go over your lessons for each pole and give thanks for your beautiful and sacred space.

Let us say you are like me and don't have a tipi in your back yard. I live in a town house and it would be difficult to build one that I could sit in comfortably and perform ceremony. I travel to a friend's barn and perform ceremony inside in colder months. What I do when blessing the barn, and you can do this for a house, is first perform a smudge on myself and again to the seven directions. I then walk with tobacco four times around the barn and pray for good feelings and good blessings for all the people. At the doorway, I smudge around it and ask that nothing evil ever be allowed to enter and to keep all negative people from my ceremonies. When I enter, I place all my sacred colors in the seven directions and I build a good smoke from the smudge bowl and allow the smoke to fill the barn/house, I then drum and chant and pray. When my prayers have been said, I take a prayer stick for ceremony and place it near or over the door. This prayer stick for especially for ceremony can have bits of different herbs tied to it, a mix of all the colors, along with feathers and crystals.

Note: There are many books on how to build a tipi but you can also advertise in your local papers, and travel to any reserves that are near you and ask if there are any workshops on building a tipi.

Sacred Fire Ritual

This is how I build a fire, first I find my spot where I want to have a fire and then I smudge the area, then me and offer smudge smoke to the seven directions.

Each stone that encircles the fire has a teaching and so similar to when building a tipi, place your beliefs into those stones for they will remember them and be a beacon for your prayers and beliefs. Sweep the rocks and all the land around with a bough of cedar or another evergreen such as pine, keep praying for good people to come to your fire, and healing to come and also love to be present around it. Then burn these evergreens in the fire pit and as the smoke rises up to the Creator chant and drum giving thanks that the trees are praying for you, that the rocks are praying for you and protecting you and this space forever. Whenever you build a fire do this.

Feasting Your Drum

Requirements:
Cloth for your drum
Herbs for blessing of the drum
A spirit bowl for your drum
Food for the feast

This ceremony starts with a feast, invite your friends or do it alone but before you eat you must first feed your drum. Take some foods from your feast, place it in the spirit bowl, and put it beside your drum. Make sure your drum is placed on a cloth, as it should never be set on the bare ground. This spirit bowl now belongs to the drum and only to be used for ceremonial purposes.

Feed your drum whenever you feel the need to do it or at least once a year making it the drum's birthday.

Never let someone you don't trust or a stranger hold your drum.

Thank the spirits who have come to the drum and always surround it with white light.

We ask our ancestors, the creepers and crawlers, the two-legged and four-legged, swimmers and winged ones to come to us and assist us in our prayers. We know that the wind has a voice and we ask the great winds of each direction to carry our prayers, songs and music to the Great Mystery, the Creator.

Before you begin drumming, smudge the area, then yourself and then offer smoke to the seven directions in the usual way. If you can't use smoke then offer an herb to the seven directions and then leave it on Mother Earth.

If you are blessing a drum to be used by the group, start in the eastern direction moving sunwise so each person gets to drum once on the drum .Then beat in unity.

If alone, beat it once and give a prayer of thanks then slowly start to beat out a song, stop and sprinkle some herbs onto it, then start to beat your drum again. Watch what direction most of the herbs are drawn to, if the herbs gather to the south then you know that your drum's sacred direction is south and the Earth Teacher and element that you honor in that direction is working with your drum. Let us say south is the direction of your drum, this means that when you are playing your drum, you should do so in the southern direction or at least acknowledge that direction, the Earth Teacher and element first before a ceremony. Do this by playing just a couple of beats in this direction and say a quick prayer of thanks. Honor this direction, the sacred color, the Earth Teacher and the element you have for it.

Now back to feasting your drum. Anoint your drum on all four sides with holy water, moon water, olive oil, or whatever resonates with you.

Give thanks to the kind of animal skin on the drum, give thanks to the kind of wood that is used.

In each direction play your drum and recite these prayers:

(Turn to the east): *Great Winds of the east the messengers of the Creator, place of the rising sun, take our prayers to the Great Mystery, source of all life. Ask for opportunities for us to prosper, for confidence, for joy and hope in our life.*

(Turn to the south): *Great Winds messengers of the South a place of warmth and growth take our prayers to the Great Mystery the source of all creation. Ask for protection, love, peace, and prosperity.*

(Turn to the west): *Great Winds messengers of the West the place of the setting sun take our prayers to the Great Mystery the source of all life, we ask to appreciate and to know the ending of cycles in our lives we know that the ending is as important as the beginning.*

(Turn to the north): *Great Winds messengers of the North where the air is cool and the frost gathers on trees. We ask you to take our prayers to the Great Mystery source of all creation, we ask for protection, strength, endurance.*

(I keep drumming while finishing my praying): *Creator's love is above me, the Creator love is within me, and love of the Creator guards my path.*

If you plan to paint the drum, try to use an oil based or natural product.

Leave the food from the spirit bowl out overnight then dispose of it by burying it in Mother Earth, or by leaving it to the birds, or offering it to a river or fire.

Treat your drum with great respect, as the drum is now a being.

A chant you could sing in this ceremony is the Mother Earth

Chant, Spiral Chant or Cherokee Morning Chant (which can be found at the end of the book).

A Baby Blessing Ceremony

Before we get started, you should be aware of some things. It is my belief that a soul decides when they are coming into this world. They consider the season, what Mother Earth is transforming into, the moon phase and much more than I could ever realize. Take a moment to reflect upon what is going on in nature at the time of the baby's birth. What phase is the moon in? What herbs and plants are plentiful? What are Mother Earth's creatures doing? Are some migrating? Storing up for winter or giving birth?

If the moon is waxing perhaps this child's path is going to be about learning to expand and grow, if the moon is waning perhaps this child will have a path that has more options for letting go then someone else. If you have moon totems look at the totem for the month the child is born. In the particular season, which element is strongest?

Try to incorporate some of this into your ritual. I will give you an example of a baby blessing I hope you can make it your own with your own special touches.

Beginning of the ceremony

The area of the ceremony is blessed with prayers and smudging. The two altars at the sides of the entrance of the circle are set up and blessed.

Everyone is smudged before entering the circle. Once everyone is inside the ceremonial area, there is an opening prayer and an invocation for protection for the circle.

Take your wand, prayer stick or broom and point it in the east and begin to turn clockwise and pray:

In the east, south, west and north

A perfect circle casts love and hope
A perfect circle casts out fear and pain
We gather here tonight to raise the vibration of positivity and power
Come all; you are invited to this sacred space.
We have come here to celebrate ..... (whatever ceremony it is)

Then everyone holds their broom or each other's hands and walk three times sunwise in a circle this signifies turning of the yearly wheel.

Suggested chant: Spiral Chant or Cherokee Morning Chant (which can be found at the end of the book).

Stop, while the Circle Keeper says a prayer.

We ask for the God and Goddess's blessings over this gathering
(Face east): *Great Spirit of Light place of the rising sun*
Let there be light on our paths, let our fire always burn brightly with love and compassion. We thank you for the gift of fire.
(Face south): *Great Spirit of Love; fill our cups with your sacred waters. We thank you for water, it is the lifeblood of Mother Earth and it sustains our lives and all life on this planet. We thank you for the gift of water.*
(Face west): *Great Spirit of Life; thank you for our bodies thank you for our paths, never let us forget our connection to Mother Earth and our connection to spirit. Thank you for the gift of earth.*
(Face north): *Thank you Great Spirit for the Creation of the universe and souls. Thank you for the air we breathe, thank you for the winds of creation — the four winds from the four kingdoms. Thank you for the messages they bring to us. We thank you for the gift of air.*
May the gifts of nature and blessings of the wise sustain us this night and throughout our lives.

Baby Eve was born June 1st, so her moon is the strawberry moon and so we will have a strawberry theme altar and/or snacks of strawberries afterwards. We held this ceremony indoors but if you are outdoors and having a fire you would enter through the gates and stand around a fire.

Here is an example:

We are indoors and standing around a table with one candle, strawberries and all the elements are displayed.

The person conducting the blessing lights the blessing candle. A prayer is said over the candle as follows:

This candle is lit with love.

The person holds the child and welcomes the child into the family of humanity and to their new home on Mother Earth:

We pray that this child will always walk in love and kindness and that their path is sacred in tune with nature.

The host then sweeps their hand over the flame of the candle and then sweeps it over the child:

By the passion of fire may this child have the gift of creativity for when the earth burns new growth comes, we pray for positive healthy growth in this child.

Then the host sweeps their hand over a crystal or a plant then over the baby's head:

By the steadiness of earth may this child have the gift of being grounded and responsible.

The host sweeps their hand over water and then over the child's head:

By the perception of water, we ask for the gift intuitiveness and insight so that this child will be wise and follow the pure road.

Finally, the host selects a feather and sweeps it over the child's head:

We ask for the gift of air to bless this child with a healthy mind and good intellect.

This follows with a chanting of the elements such as the Spiral Chant and everyone leaves the circle through the blessed gates.

Prayer Stick Ceremonies

There are so many variables for making prayer sticks, some say that there should be two sticks one for male energy the other for female energy, some say the bark should be stripped off some say it shouldn't.

The sticks shared here are my prayer sticks made my way and used in ceremony the way I prefer but I hope you make your own sticks based on what you like and have fun with them. I make prayer sticks because I love trees, they give us shade and they give us food like maple syrup yummy! And they bring oxygen to our planet and much more.

I select trees that I feel drawn to. Next, I offer some tobacco to the tree for allowing me to use its branch for a ritual. When choosing your wood, try to find fallen branches. I like to bless them and decorate them with items that are spiritual and then infuse them with the intention of protection and blessings. Here is my ceremony that I perform when preparing my sticks for myself and/or gifts to friends.

You can substitute the sticks for a bolline, athame, broom or wand it just depends on what you feel comfortable using and what you are drawn to. If you prefer brooms, you can buy small brooms in craft stores, which are perfect.

Prayer Stick Ceremony East

East — air, communication, new beginnings, new growth

Shh... Grandmother Cedar holds many secrets

Before I begin, I make this gesture and affirmation. I take my prayer stick in my left hand and draw the Celtic cross starting above my head I point my broom/wand upward and whisper *The Divine Creator*. I bring my prayer stick to the ground and say *Mother Earth*. I then go to the left of my body holding my stick I say *Sacred Door Keepers*. I bring my stick to the right of me and say *Sacred Earth Teachers*. Lastly, I make a circle and say *Sacred Circle of Life*. I lay my prayer stick down on a cloth and take another deep breath and stretch my arms out to form a cross. I say this prayer:

> *I stand, in the center of this sacred circle with arms outstretched in a pose of gratitude. I arise today through the power of the Creation that supports me, blesses me and heals me. I give thanks for my life and for nature and I humbly ask for Divine guidance in my life. May there be beauty above me, beauty within me and beauty below me.*

My direction here is the east and my color here is as usual yellow. This color is affixed to my prayer stick. The Earth Teacher here is cedar; the Door Keeper is the Archangel Gabriel. The journey is east to the Divine; this means I need to connect with the Source of Creation to give thanks for all I have and for my home Mother Earth. Earth Teacher cedar is an evergreen, her needles honor the four seasons, her strength can carry you through life's situations her medicine is peaceful and nurturing. Cedar purifies and cleanses areas. Make a wreath of cedar to protect your home. I depend on her wisdom and power to draw divine energy down into myself. Celtic and the Aboriginals of North America have valued cedar as a tree of protection and healing.

Angels are God's and Goddess's expression of love and cedar is a great source of Vitamin C.

The Earth Teacher cedar is known as the Tree of Life, this tree cleanses negative energies from the environment. It is a joyous tree, its energy is pure bliss and happiness; it promotes feelings of peace and tranquility. It is very grounding and so it is an excellent tool in drawing the divine, but also in keeping us grounded so we can focus on being more creative and bringing new opportunities into our lives.

God our Father and Goddess our Mother.
In a wonderful way, you guide the work of angels and humans.
May those who serve you constantly in heaven.
Keep our lives safe from all harm on earth.

Attach something yellow to your cedar prayer stick to pay homage to your sacred color and the sacred element of this direction, which is air. You can also attach crystals, feathers (for the air element) angels and so forth.

Decorate it as you please. The more you put into your prayer stick the stronger it is. My prayer stick hangs inside my home on the eastern side. I have charged my stick with the intention of bringing blessings into my home. I also pray that my prayer stick brings in new growth and creativity such as ideas of careers, life paths, expressions of self and wisdom from the Great Spirit.

Facing east with my prayer stick in both hands I first acknowledge what direction I am facing and the sacred color which is yellow, and the element of air. At this moment, I take some time to show reverence and respect to the materials that went into my prayer stick. A take a couple of deep and cleansing breaths and meditate on what I want to draw into my life. I allow my mind to relax, taking in a deep breath again and imagine I am breathing in the pure yellow power of this world.

Now it's time to connect with my Door Keeper, the Archangel

Gabriel. I close my eyes and visualize the sun rising in the east; the golden glow of the sun fills my body and my prayer stick with its warmth. I feel secure and strong like a cedar tree, rooted to the warm earth I imagine myself as a tree standing in the warm sunshine on a summer day very rooted to the ground and secure of my natural place in the universe.

I visualize the Archangel Gabriel standing beside me; he is a beautiful large angel glowing with the light of Goddess/God. I make myself aware of his guidance in my life and how completely protected I am. I give thanks to God for my protection and I give thanks to this incredibly beautiful angel for protecting me and guiding me.

Angels are our precious friends.

I bring my prayer stick to my chest, as I am holding it, I ask the angel to empower this stick with the power to bring positive changes and new growth into my life. I pray:

Sacred trees I hear your songs in the wind, and it eases my pain, show me the spiritual medicine of healing herbs and my natural connection to nature, I pray that these prayer sticks will protect my home and help my spiritual walk with the Creator, teach me to walk the path of respect and honor for Mother Earth. Sacred trees heal my heart so I can see the gift you offer. Angels help my prayers.

I offer herbs to my smudge bowl or fire, as the smoke rises I pass my stick through the smoke cleansing it and tuning it to the angelic forces. Now my prayer stick is charged and ready to be used. Cedar helps our prayers. Cree people call cedar trees Grandmothers, for they are older and wiser then we are.

Note: The trees of this ceremony have natural balance and while the trees are rooted to the earth, they don't need to be cleansed.

Using the sticks in clearing or releasing negative energies in people and places will result in the sticks need to be renewed and restored to their natural balance. It is a good idea to periodically to this ritual to refresh and re-energize your prayer sticks. Then the trees of the forest will sing, they will sing for joy before the Creator.

Prayer Stick Ceremony South

South — fire, energy, passion, creativity

Druids believe humans descended from trees

A seed hidden in the heart of an apple is an orchard invisible.
~Welsh Proverb

South, my spiritual direction is outward which means what I am putting out into this world is going to be a blessing or a hindrance. My color here is black, my Earth Teacher is the Apple Tree and my Door Keeper is Archangel Raphael.

Holding my prayer stick made from apple wood in my hand, I take a moment to connect with my Door Keeper Archangel Raphael. I focus on my prayers and invocations for help and blessings. I visualize deep rich jewel tones of color wrapped around me in love and protection. I ask this sacred messenger of the Creator God to renew my energy, keep my connection with my loved ones strong and to bring love and creativity into my life. Archangel Raphael is the angel of soul mates, marriages, healing and travel, his name means 'medicine of God'. I evoke his power to help me with issues of relationships, physical healing, and ties to my ancestors.

Our Father Creator,
In a wonderful way you guide the work of angels and humans...
May those who serve you constantly in the heavens

Keep our lives safe from all harm on earth.

The Earth Teacher in this ritual is Apple Tree. The Druids believe that the apple tree has mystical powers, now we enjoy her fruits throughout the long winter months. This tree teaches me to save and to be prepared for the winter in my life. So start a savings account, put those coins away for a rainy day, this is a lesson of the apple tree.

Archangel Raphael along with the Apple Tree teaches me to open my heart to abundance, to trust Father in times of lack, but keep a healthy balance of saving and giving. When I do give, I should do it with an open heart knowing that the Creator can replenish me through Mother Earth.

I hold my prayer stick in my hand with the desire to connect with this marvelous wood, I want to understand psyche of this tree, I smell my prayer stick breathing in the essence of its energy. Holding my prayer stick, I program it to attract soul mates/kindred spirits into my life, to connect me to my ancestors and allow the healing forces within me to be released. I ask Archangel Raphael to shine the light of the Creator onto my prayer stick.

The trees are God's great alphabet:
With them, He writes in shining green
across the world His thoughts serene.
~Leonora Speyer

Facing south with wand in my hands I first acknowledge, what direction I am facing, then I say my sacred color in this direction which is black, then the Door Keeper's name which is Archangel Raphael, then my Earth Teacher which is Apple Tree. I ask my Door Keeper to protect my prayers and send them to the Divine. I bring my prayer stick to my chest, holding it, I ask the angel to empower this prayer stick with the ability to attract soul mates and bring healing forces into my life. I pray:

Sacred trees I hear your songs in the wind, and it eases my pain, show me the spiritual medicine of healing herbs and my natural connection to nature. I pray that these prayer sticks will protect my home and help my spiritual walk with the Creator. Teach me to walk the path of respect and honor for Mother Earth. Sacred trees heal my heart so I can see the gift you offer. Holy Angel help my prayers.

I offer sage to my smudge bowl or fire, as the smoke rises I pass my prayer stick through the smoke cleansing it and tuning it to the angelic forces.

Now my prayer stick is charged and ready to be used.

Prayer Stick Ceremony West

West = water, emotion, psyche, movement

There's a shining tree in my soul

Stand still. The trees ahead and the bush beside you are not lost.
~Albert Einstein

West, my color here is red; I have this color affixed to my prayer stick. The Earth Teacher here is Willow, and my Door Keeper is Archangel Ariel, I take a moment to connect with the angel of this direction. I take a deep breath and ask Archangel Ariel to help me; I promise myself that I will treasure this angelic assistance in my life.

Our Father Creator,
in a wonderful way you guide the work of angels and humans...
May those who serve you constantly in heaven
keep our lives safe from all harm on earth.

The journey is inward to the Divine; this means I need to connect with my soul to understand others and myself. I then do this meditation. I visualize a ball of light within my chest, this ball of light is eternal, and it has all the wisdom of the universe within it. I take my time creating this glorious orb its incandescence glows as it slowly unfurls its beauty within me. I watch in awe, its perfection spins and rotates effortlessly. Ripples of light swirl around me, I allow this orb to envelope me with its beauty and softness, caressing my skin, this is love. Love enfolds me, love sustains me, and love supports me. This is my ancient self; this is the kingdom of God within. It is here that I travel to when life confuses me. I ask Archangel Ariel to encompass me in God's love.

Better than a thousand hollow words, is one word that brings peace
~Buddha

Now I focus onto Earth Teacher Willow. She eases our pains; her bark contains properties that diminishes inflammation and promote healing. The Creator designed her flowing limbs to be a refuse for animals and people. She is a safe haven to us during stormy times. Grandmother Willow heals our emotions she teaches us to bend with life and to surrender what cannot be changed to the Creator. The willow represents love, healing, protection, and is especially powerful for women.

Facing west with wand in my hands, I acknowledge what direction I am facing, the sacred color, Earth Teacher Willow and my Door Keeper Archangel Ariel.

I then take a moment to think of the willow tree and its energies. Holding my prayer stick, I feel one with the ancient wisdom of creation. I bring my prayer stick to my chest, holding it, I ask the angel to empower this stick with ability to attract feelings of empowerment and expertise in all that I do. To strengthen my intuitive skills and allow me to feel and know things what was hidden to me.

Sage is what I offer to the smudge bowl or fire. As the smoke raises up I pass my stick through the smoke to cleanse it, I say a prayer of thanks to earth mother for my prayer stick. My tool is now ready to protect and promote positivity in my life.

There is always Music amongst the trees in the Garden, but our hearts must be very quiet to hear it.
~Minnie Aumonier

Prayer Stick Ceremony North

North = earth, home, security, fertility

Pine, burn it for strength, and to reverse negative energies.

North, my spiritual direction here is downward, which means in this direction I am reminded to stay focused on my path in life, Door Keeper is Archangel Michael, sacred color here is white, and Earth Teacher is pine.

Father with great wisdom. You direct the ministry of Angels and men. Grant that those who always minister to You in heaven may defend us during our life on earth. Amen

Holding my prayer stick made from pine in my hand, I take time to connect with my Door Keeper Archangel Michael; I visualize his wings wrapped around me in protection. I feel the firmness of his strength and authority; I make a silent vow to myself to honor this sacred connection. I ask St Michael to watch over my home and all matters related to my security, to assist me in my finances and to help me attain my goals. I ask him to bless my home and my prayer stick.

Then I close my eyes and picture a beautiful ball of luminous energy above my head I watch as the ball opens, angelic light cascades all over me. I am illuminated in a radiant splendor of heavenly light; this light moves throughout my body and forms a protective bubble that keeps me safe from negative energies.

Remember to surround your prayer stick in the white light and the better you can imagine the light the stronger your results will be.

Our treasures lie within our hearts

The Earth Teacher here is pine, this is an evergreen, its old title is 'the sweetest of woods' and its needles are a great source of vitamin C. The scent of pine is useful in alleviating stress and worries. I take a couple of deep cleansing breaths and allow my mind to relax, I meditate on the pine tree. I feel the energy of this tree in my hands; I imagine I am breathing in the pure natural power of this tree. Smelling my stick I welcome the pine scent, twirling it slowly in my fingers I put my intentions into my stick. I program my prayer stick to rebel adverse energies, attract positive activity such as financial prosperity and to keep me on the right path in life. I ask Archangel Michael to shine the light of the Creator on my prayer stick.

Druids claimed pine was the 'the sweetest of woods.'

Pine needles are good sources of vitamin C

Facing north with my prayer stick in my hand, I acknowledge what direction I am facing, the color, the Door Keeper and Earth Teacher. I bring my stick to my chest, holding it, I ask the angel to empower this prayer stick with the power to attract abundance and prosperity into my life. I pray:

Sacred trees I hear your songs in the wind, and it eases my pain, show me the spiritual medicine of healing herbs and my natural connection to nature, I pray that these prayer sticks will protect my home and help my spiritual walk with the Creator, teach me to walk the path of respect and honor for Mother Earth. Sacred trees heal my heart so I can see the gift you offer. Angels help my prayers.

I offer herbs to my smudge bowl or fire, as the smoke rises I pass my stick through the smoke cleansing it and tuning it to the angelic forces.

Now my prayer stick is charged and ready to be used.

Decorate your prayer stick as you please but make sure your sacred color is shown in some fashion, such as in this direction you could attach blue angel wings. This prayer stick will hang on my northern side of my home; its energy will protect my family and me.

Chapter Five

The Moon – Esbats

Grandmother Moon

There is something magical about a full moon; her timeless beauty beckons to us to come out and play under her bewitching glow. Moonlight offers us a reprieve from the warmth of Grandfather Sun. Nokum's glow is cooler and softer her medicine is quieter, in her knowledge she remembers our connections to others. For centuries lovers have fallen victim to her allure and you shall to if you dare to wander about some starry night being ready for whatever the moonlight has to offer. Under her hypnotic luster, we feel like we are ethereal beings, timeless, aware of our spiritual bodies. Grandmother Moon watches us with curiosity, she marvels at the depths we can travel too in the name of love and hate. I wonder how long has Grandmother looked upon tortured souls and have felt their pain ... that is part of her wisdom, she watches us.

In the moonlight, I feel connected to the mysteries of this world, to the old people, to the spirits of the night. I am very aware that I am a part of something veiled and mystical. The old stories I relished as a young woman of witches, wizards, and creatures of the night flood my mind with fantastical images.

Primordial memories of bonfires dotted along an ancient landscape tug at my spirit. Suddenly I am surrounded by my ancestors celebrating an older knowledge that I have forgotten, but not lost. The lure here is strong ... like the tides that are controlled by the moon, she also has the power to tug at my soul, and she transports me back in time ... back in time to a place of magic and power.

Some have muttered this is sinful; this is dangerous, we

remember our fallen ancestors who lost their lives in the name of spiritual freedom. It is important to remember and to honor the power of Nokum our Grandmother. The message of the missionaries is fading, there scare tactics don't work on us anymore, we have evolved to where we no longer fear the darkness, we remember our people. Our ancestors have waited so long to teach us, to hold us, to help us on our path. They know 'their' truths are powerful, in the shadows they wait for us, they understand ritual, they understand the need to dance and drum under the moon.

This is when I love to slip on my shawl, wrapped in its softness like moonlight ... fragile yet protective as is Grandmother.

I step out into the night filled with expectation and the rush of the unknown.

She is the natural cycle of life in the night sky. The rhythm of our lives is demonstrated in the heavens. We see birth, life, death and rebirth, we are part of the universe, and we are connected. The sacred hoop of life is mirrored in Grandmother Moon's cycles. How precious is this chain of events, the unending band of life.

When I see Nokum is new I feel hopes stirring within my blood, aspirations, goals, desires flood my body. This is a woman's power time, there is something so feminine at this stage of moon time, looking up at her she is yielding, she is seductive and she is sensuous. When she is full of her glory, she is feminine power in full force for three nights she remains full of her splendor, this is when I seek my visions, and she illuminates that which is hidden inside of me. When Grandmother begins to wane I understand now that with age comes wisdom, she dismisses that which no longer serves her as I must let go of those things that hinder me ... letting go, abolishing the waste that ties me down.

I watch her beauty her cycle until she is a pale crescent in the night sky, she is older and wiser then I will ever be. She allows me to hear the echoes from the past, they linger ensnared within Mother Earth's web, but controlled by the cycles of Grandmother Moon ... murmurings spoken in shadows of the blackest hue ... remain with me. Hushed voices chanting prayers can heard if one stays quiet and listens ... these teachings are part of our knowledge that remains dormant within us ... that is until we walk under Grandmother's moonbeams were we feel the peacefulness of the night. A time of ritual and remembering those that have gone on before us.

The full moon is excellent times to connect with our Ancestors not only for asking their guidance but to also give them gifts such as feeding their spirits.

Full Moon Earth Wheel

Give thanks to our ancestors. Feeding their spirits.

Begin by smudging yourself and your area of where you will do your ceremony then arrange eight candles, eight mini electric candles or eight guards that have been carved out with a light placed within. Arrange in a circle to imitate the eight phases of the moon. These are the New Moon, Waxing Crescent, First Quarter, Waxing Gibbous, Full Moon, Waning Gibbous, Last Quarter, and Waning Crescent. Again, this is when you can use your feathers that have been cleansed and blessed. Standing inside your circle of eight lights or stones and beginning in the north (the direction in the wheel where we honor our ancestors) we offer smoke from our smudge bowl using our feathers we fan the smoke in each of the seven directions until we end up facing north again. In each direction be in a state of reverence and let there be moments of silence to honor the dead.

Before I begin, I make this gesture and affirmation. I take my prayer stick in my left hand and draw the Celtic cross starting above my head I point my broom/wand upward and whisper *The Divine Creator*. I bring my prayer stick to the ground and say *Mother Earth*. I then go to the left of my body holding my stick I say *Sacred Door Keepers*. I bring my stick to the right of me and say *Sacred Earth Teachers*. Lastly, I make a circle and say *Sacred Circle of Life*. I lay my prayer stick down on a cloth and take another deep breath and stretch my arms out to form a cross. I say this prayer:

I stand, in the center of this sacred circle with arms outstretched in a pose of gratitude. I arise today through the power of the Creation that supports me, blesses me and heals me. I give thanks for my life and for nature and I humbly ask for Divine guidance in my life. May there be beauty above me, beauty within me and beauty below me.

Take something different such as myrrh, or a mixed herb sachet and burn it, say a prayer for all your ancestors, a prayer that all souls find their peace and safety in the afterlife.

Creator we offer you this sacred herb in order of our brothers and sisters who have passed into spirit — they came from love and have returned to love. May the love we are sending out into the universe assist all who are in need, let our loving energies carry all into the light of the Divine. Earth Teacher Owl; deliver my prayers to the Creator.

Make a list of the names of loved ones and friends who are in the spirit world, and place them on your moon altar (small table in the center of your circle with smudging items and white candle). Focus your energy on the candle light and your loved ones and pray that each of them has found the light and peace of the Goddess/God, Creator. Offer up prayers on their behalf, offer up the smoke for them. Bring a flower for them or make a sachet of flowers and place your sacred colors within the sachet and a small crystal, bless this sachet or flower and offer it the earth.

The group or a person alone can make the sachet/s together then offer them to the earth either by fire, water, tying them to a tree, or burying them in the earth preferably by a tree.

Take some time in the ceremony to do some drumming and chanting.

The next phase of the ritual is optional or this can be done instead of blessing your ancestors.

Make a circle of eight candles with a center white candle and then smudge to the seven directions. In your hand, hold your moon crystal and place within this crystal everything that you want to happen in your life such as:

I will always have love in my life. I will be surrounded by kindred spirits and soul mates. I will have good health and prosperity in my life. My days upon this earth plane will be long and filled with happiness.

Holding my crystal and starting at the northern direction of my circle, I begin my journey around the circle. At each candle with my crystal, I pause and affirm my intention of what I desire. When I reach the waning part of the moon cycle, I switch my crystal there and use a new one then continue and I affirm what I want to let go of, such as weight, self-sabotage, anger and so on. When I have completed my journey, I find my seat and wait for the others to complete theirs. When everyone has finished, there is a group blessing of all the crystals followed by drumming and chanting.

Sometimes I will make up a crystal grid on my moon altar and recharge it during the full moon. A crystal grid is very easy to make but it is very powerful. The easiest grid is one that is created with five crystals using all the same type of stone; I prefer clear quartz and use stones that are very similar in size and shape.

Make a small bed of sand within a small container. Before you place in our sand, write down on a piece of paper what you desire in your life next. Cover the paper with sand then place your crystals on top, with one crystal in each corner and one in the center. Next take up a small pointed piece of quartz and draw lines in the air connecting all your crystals, visualize white light connecting all the stones. Finish the connecting in the center stone. Now your grid is charged, do this on the full moon when the energies are high.

If I'm performing my moon ritual alone, I have my altar set up with my Goddess Moon candle surrounded by thirteen grandmother moon candles, instead of walking around eight stations, I bring out my art work of the phases of the moon and use those to decorate my moon altar. When ready (after smudging ritual) I hold my crystal to my heart and make my eight affirmations. Below are two chants you could try:

Under a waning and waxing moon
The Goddess spins the wheel
Life, death and rebirth
The Goddess spins the wheel
Or
Moons of creation shine on us tonight
Moons of creation guide us through the night
Ancestors pray for us, Creator heal us
Moons of creation draw me to the Light

Often we will chant to the Spiral Chant or the Mother Earth Chant.

Herbs of the Earth Ritual

Full moon is excellent for connecting to nature

The Set Up

You will need two smaller tables containing items such as candles that have been blessed and all the elements represented in some fashion — earth, water, fire and air.

Take some sacred herbs that you have prayed over and place into dishes on either side of the table. In addition, you can have angel statues, blessed and cleansed crystals, and whatever you use as talismans for protection.

Instead of tables, you can just have large blessed candles on each side or poles decorated with herbs, feathers and crystals. The purpose of the altars is to act as a filtering station that will not allow evil to pass by. It is for your protection and your circle's protection. You may also have a center table or altar that will contain your supplies that you will need to perform the ritual, such as candles and herbs; you can also place some protective crystals around your altar.

Each person needs to bring a bowl (this will be their spirit bowl which should not be used for anything but ceremony), along with their own herbs, a clean cloth to wrap up their herb, spices, a small candle and anything else they wish to bring.

Smudge the area as before, smudge yourself and offer smudge smoke to the seven directions. Smudge all ritual items and the candles or altars that stand at the entrance of the circle.

After the smudging ritual (outside the circle), you call the people into the circle. Everyone enters with their bowls of herbs and their candles. Everyone is chanting and singing. The host can do some drumming for the group since people's hands will be holding items. Keep moving around the circle for a few turns counter clockwise, as it is a grand entry. As people are dancing, have them turn to face each other with their herbs held in the air (still chanting).

When you call a stop, people should remain standing for prayer. The host lights a candle and prays:

Within this circle tonight, we have come to share the respect and honor we have for the medicines of Mother Earth. As healers, we must show kindness and compassion wherever we go. We are created to live in love and harmony not just with each other but also with creation.

The host walks the circle saying a prayer like the one above. After the prayer is said, everyone sits and takes a clean cloth and covers up their herbs. This sacred cloth can be decorated with beads or can be plain, whatever suits the person. Next, everyone prays over their herbs with one hand holding the bowl and the other over it.

Periodically they should bring their free hand to their hearts and ask to have a holy connection with the herbs or herb. With their hearts and spirit, they ask this connection to be pure and beautiful so that they can help themselves, their families, communities, and animals of this earth.

The host takes everyone on a guided meditation to connect with their herb or spice. A simple meditation begins with everyone holding their bowls of herbs and with both feet on the ground. They should take a couple of deep relaxing breaths and focus the mind gently on the herbs in the bowl. Feel what kind of energy the plant radiates; is it feminine or masculine? Are the plant people friendly or not? What color surrounds the herb? They should imagine themselves drinking the herb; ask where does the energy of the herb flow to in the body? Imagine the energy of the herb sparkles and attaches itself to areas of the body it helps. Breathe in the essence of the herbs how does it *feel* inside the body. These are simple meditations to start with you can get more in depth each time the circle meets. Do some research on psychometry and practice it on herbs and medicines.

Prayer is said to the Creator and Mother Earth, such as this one:

We dance tonight to heal the earth and in healing our mother, we heal ourselves. Creator and Mother Earth please accept our humble offerings tonight. Great Spirit hear the prayers of your people tonight, you are our way in this circle of life.

After the prayer, the people attending should offer the herbs. They don't have to burn them all but can burn a small amount. However, if they are toxic offer them outside wrapped in the cloth and buried or placed somewhere safe where people won't walk on them. Alternatively wrap them in the cloth and hang them outside somewhere like in a tree. We want our offering to be joined to the earth, air, water or fire.

If people had to go outside to do this then afterwards all come back to rejoin the circle and stand in prayer.

When everyone is back inside the circle and remember they enter through the blessed gates, do some singing and dancing. Perform some side steps around the circle and chant some more, after a few minutes everyone sits down. The host sprinkles each person with an herbal mixture and prays for each person that they will do their best as healers and they will always have that deep connection to their herbs and remedies.

The herbal mixture should be something like spearmint, dandelion or lavender, remember that if you are inside, these herbs will have to be swept up or vacuumed then dispose of the herbs back to the earth and not put in a garbage can.

Each person arises and lights their candles from the candle on the main altar and then there is a group prayer or oath is taken to treat the earth and medicines with respect.

An example of a group prayer or oath could go something like this:

Father I see you in the flight of an eagle, Mother I feel you under my feet, I feel your heart beat. Creator never allow us to lose our way heal the healer so that we can be a healing force to others. Within this circle may we be granted wisdom; within this circle may we form a bond with our medicines. From within this circle may we be given peace and leave with your peace.

The candles are blown out at once and with the breath of the people, the prayers rise up to the Creator. Drumming and singing leaving the circle, the Grand exit

You can adjust this ceremony for a solitary person; do your prayers, chanting, drumming, singing and offerings in the same fashion.

Gypsy Moon Ceremony

Items you will need for this ritual.

Depending on the number of people, you will have to have at least two decks of playing cards.
A booklet for the definition of the cards.
Smudge sticks such as sage or sweet grass.
Items for your altars.
Candles and items from the earth representing the elements.
You will require an assistant to help.

The Set Up
Two smaller tables containing items such as blessed candles. All the elements represented in some fashion should be on the table, (earth, water, fire and air). Place some sacred herbs that you have prayed over in dishes on either side of the table.

Angel statues blessed and cleansed crystals, whatever you use as talismans for protection. Instead of tables, you can just have large blessed candles on each side or poles decorated with herbs, feathers and crystals.

The purpose of the altars is to act as a filtering station that will not allow evil to pass by. It is for your protection and your circle's protection.

You will need a center table or altar that will contain your supplies, which you will need to perform the ritual and placed on it candles and herbs. You can place some protective crystals around your table.

In the eastern, southern, western, northern sections of your circle, put small tables that will hold your playing cards. Each suit of the deck resonates with a direction in your circle as follows. Spades are air and east; Clubs are fire and south; Hearts are water and west; and finally Diamonds are earth and north.

On the eastern table take all the clubs out of the deck and place them on that table. Do this with all the tables until the decks are all divided amongst the tables. You will want many cards from which the people can select. On your center altar you should have enough representations of the elements for each table, so have a couple of feathers, a bowl of water or some shells, a crystal or dish of earth and an extra candle an extra crystal that resonates with the fire element such as fire agate. You will need this because you will be calling up someone to carry elements to each corner of the circle. You will need a candle for each direction as well in addition to the seven candles for your own table.

The ritual opens with the smudging ceremony. Smudge your area, smudging self and others and offer the smudge smoke to the seven directions.

People enter a gate of candles or altar filled with blessed items that has been placed on either side of the entrance of circle. Don't forget to smudge the candles or altars.

Once everything has been smudged, call the people into the circle. People enter the circle with drumming and singing. Allow people to sing going counter clockwise around the circle a few times, this brings up the energy of the circle. Once the singing has ended the people stand in a circle around the center table.

Light seven candles: the first is for good fortune, the second is for healing, the third is for love, the fourth is for luck, the fifth is for protection, the sixth is for friendships which is pure and the seventh is for guidance from the cards tonight.

Then drum some more and sing and a song as you move around the circle.

Chants such as Mother Earth Chant and the Spiral Chant are all excellent chants for this ceremony.

An assistant should light a candle on the first table with the spades on it. Remember to move counter clockwise wise. Discuss the element of air and its meanings. When doing this it could be an added feature to look at the month you are in and what astrological sign the moon is in and talk about how that relates to the group. For example if you are in October the moon would be in Scorpio, read up on the characteristics of that influence and fit that into how the mood of that energy could affect the energy of the circle.

The host's assistant stands by the first table that has cards on it, the host calls for people to come and select a card from the table.

After the host explains each table's contents people are called up to select a card from that table. This is done so people can mediate for a moment on the cards. For example, before I select a club from the club table, I will think about issues that surround non-emotional things such as work, education, activities such as exercise.

This is done in each of the four corners. There should be a teaching on the suits their elements and how it relates to us while the cards are selected.

Let's do a brief recap. The host's assistant stands by the first table, which has cards on it. The host calls for people to come and select a card from the table. When everyone has selected a card from that table, the circle moves again and chants and dances perhaps once or twice around the circle. The host talks about the cards on the next table and calls for people to select a card (dancing around once again). Everyone moves onto the next table until each person has one card from each table.

When all cards are selected, the host stops and says a prayer of thanks and asks that the Gypsy Moon will give good messages tonight.

The assistant leads the group out through the blessed gates, singing and chanting the grand exit.

The host closes the circle and puts out the candles.

Over tea and snacks, the people from the group read up on what their cards mean.

Full Moon Animal Totem Ritual

For this example, I will use owl medicine (one of the full moons).

Owl Moon — *Fellowship of the winged ones*

I smudge my ceremonial area, all my items for ritual, myself, and offer smoke to the seven directions.

Before I begin, I make this gesture and affirmation. I take my prayer stick in my left hand and draw the Celtic cross starting above my head I point my broom/wand upward and whisper *The Divine Creator*. I bring my prayer stick to the ground and say *Mother Earth*. I then go to the left of my body holding my stick I say *Sacred Door Keepers*. I bring my stick to the right of me and say *Sacred Earth Teachers*. Lastly, I make a circle and say *Sacred Circle of Life*. I lay my prayer stick down on a cloth and take another deep breath and stretch my arms out to form a cross. I say this prayer:

I stand, in the center of this sacred circle with arms outstretched in a pose of gratitude. I arise today through the power of the Creation that supports me, blesses me and heals me. I give thanks for my life and for nature and I humbly ask for Divine guidance in my life. May there be beauty above me, beauty within me and beauty below me.

I light my moon candle then I ring my bell this lets spirit know that I am about to before a ceremony.

Great Spirit we offer your sacred resin to the fire, please hear the prayers of your grandchild enter my circle and infuse me with your peace and strength.

Owl sounds like the wind WHOooo.

I will chant now using one of the chants from the back of the book.

I stand at my altar and I turn with my feather (or an item relating to owl) in my hand and cross my hands over my heart. I take a moment to connect with the item I am holding, to sense how this bird was part of the ecosystem.

The color here I acknowledge is brown. The Earth Teacher is Owl; I ask myself what is there about the owl that the Creator uses to teach me about life? Owls are solitary and quiet creatures; they have keen powers of observation. They desire to learn and analyze what goes on around them; they see their prey in the dark and can swoop in and get what they want. The Owl teaches me that even when fear whispers to me that the night is too dark, the Owl reminds me that the Creator can overcame the power of the dark through the Owl.

A wise old Owl sat on an oak. The more he saw the less he spoke.

The less he spoke the more he heard.

Why aren't we all like that wise old bird-Nursery Rhyme?

I stand at my altar with my item in my hand and pray:

> *Great Spirit I offer your sacred herbs to the fire, please hear the prayers of your grandchild. I stand as your granddaughter/grandson within this sacred hoop and ask you to bless my relatives, the four legged, and two legged, the swimmers, the winged ones, the creepers and the crawlers. Great Spirit let me always have an open mind and a willingness to learn from you and all the creatures of this world and from Mother Earth herself. The four winds of the earth messengers of the Creator take my prayers to the Great Spirit and to Mother Earth.*

I give thanks to the Great Spirit for my Earth Teacher owl. I offer sage to the smudge bowl or fire, as the smoke rises up I pass my item through the smoke to be cleansed.

After the cleansing of the item, I place it where it will be held on my altar and then will do some chanting perhaps some dancing. This is a sacred night for my totem and me. In the coming days I will want to learn about this animal or creature in order to help me go grow into a better wiser human being. With a deep inhale I breathe in my prayers for a beautiful connection with nature and with my exhale I blow out my ceremonial candles and with my breath I send my requests and thanksgiving to the Great Mystery.

I chose brown to be my sacred color that will be associated with my owl totem, so I like to wear brown or have a brown cloth on my altar for the ceremony.

New Moon Herb Totem Ritual

The world is within me

Herbs spring forth from the womb of our Mother

Many people think of animals when someone talks about totems and there are animal totems but you can have herb totems as well. Take myself for example; I resonate easier and more intimately with herbs and plants than animals. I can tune into herbs and plants and they speak to me, they will tell me how they feel about people, how they want to work with people or not work with people. They will let me know how they feel and work with other herbs.

When I tune into or link with sweet grass this plant tells me that it calls to other plants to come and work with it to perform the intention required of it. For an example if you'd like to use rosemary for protection, I feel that when I connect with this plant it really doesn't want to perform this action but when I ask sweet grass to ask rosemary to protect, it does so. I will take a braid of sweet grass, lay it with rosemary, and say prayers over them both asking for the herbs to drive away all evil spirits.

Now back to my full moon herbal totem ceremony, this ritual is for requesting an herb to work with myself for a certain project, a moon cycle, or for life.

I like to use sweet grass to smudge with because this plant calls to other plants to help. I smudge the area, others and myself if I am not alone. I then offer the smudge smoke to the seven directions. Interesting to note here about sweet grass, after the braid has been lit it doesn't call out to other plants while it is being used to smudge; it focuses on the job at hand.

On my table or altar I will have a bowl of herbs of the ones I want to connect with, three candles (you can use scented ones). The first candle is for Mother Earth and her elements and all her plants and herbs, the second one is for the herb or essential oil and the third is for me. All the elements will represented in some fashion such as a shell for water, soil or salt for earth, candle for fire and feather for air.

Sit in a comfortable position alone or in a circle and say a prayer something like this: light the first candle and say a prayer for the second and third candles. Do a protection meditation. First, imagine yourself in the bag of light. Pure, white light is surrounding you and radiating from you. Ask loved ones and your guides to stand in protection for yourself.

The rhythms of my body are the rhythms of my mother's body

Then do a connection visualization and meditation with the herb or essential oil. The purpose of this exercise is to develop psychometry skills using plants and herbs. Psychometry is an intuitive skill at holding an object and gathering information from it. What I discovered is an inanimate object doesn't speak to you, but a living plant does. Using this method you can have almost like a dialogue with the herb.

Hold the herb in your hand, feel the emotions from this plant, allow your mind to rest and allow images around the herb to materialize in your mind's eye. What colors around the plant to you see or sense and ask those colors what they mean. Ask the herb questions such as, 'do you want to work with people? 'Do you feel protective of the space you are in?' and 'How do you heal the body?' Then imagine yourself drinking a tea made from the herb, how does the fluid affect your body, where does the energy of the liquid travel to and what does it do there. Ask the herb how much should I take or when should I take you. Gather all your information and then research your findings and compare it to your text books.

Remember always speak to your doctor and a certified herbalist before you embark on any treatment.

This exercise can be done with your herbal teas you drink on a regular basis such as peppermint.

Finish the ritual with drumming and chanting.

Your fragrant grasses and flowers are your hair

New Moon Crystal Healing Ceremony

The new moon is for making and blessing offering stones.

The world is within me

This ceremony actually begins a few days before the new moon. During the phase of the dark moon take some time to connect with nature, either by walking, taking a drive in the country, meditating to some nature sounds, whichever you choose.

Set up a table with some items from the elements, such as a container of soil or something from the earth, bowl of water, candle or a feather to represent air and an object that represents your spirituality such as a statue of an angel.

Make yourself comfortable and hold each one and feel your connection to it.

I think of the earth as I hold my dirt. I imagine rocks, trees, bricks, buildings but I also think of my own building my teeth, my bones, my cartilage and so forth. I want to connect with everything that is of the earth element not just in the world but that, which is in me as well. The earth element is flowing through me all the time.

I set my dirt aside and hold my bowl of water. I think of oceans, seas, lakes, rivers, drops of water, my teardrops, my blood, my saliva and all the liquid that is inside me. I am water. The water flows through me, I will return to the earth someday.

Now I pick up my candle and gaze into the flame. I think of

the sun and the power of it. I think of the lightening and how it is a part of creating life. Fire is the molten core of our planet. I think of the fire element that inside me the heat of my body, the electrical impulses that are firing in my brain. I am part of the fire but I don't own it. It flows through me.

I then take up my feather and think of the atmosphere of the planet, the clouds, wind and the feeling of breezes on my skin, the sounds of wind in the trees and I briefly focus on my breathing. The simple act of breathing the breath is what is keeping me alive, air moves through me and it gives me life.

I do think of my spirit as an element, my spirit allows me to experience and be a part of this world. During this small meditation I notice how each of the elements were affecting me, which one did I feel more drawn to and I make my choice of what element I would like to work with during the next moon phase. Shortly before my ceremony, I like to start my mediations on what element is willing to work with me during the next moon phase. I am not worshiping the element — I am working with it.

This is a ritual for self-healing and for charging crystals to heal or bring protection for myself and/or others.

The yellow calcite draws me into her yellow beauty. I hold this crystal and place my intentions into it such as losing weight, and having more willpower in eating a healthier diet. Since I have felt drawn to the fire element I like to cleanse my crystal in the sunshine (be careful not to place a crystal ball in the sun as it can pose a fire threat).

The night of the ritual, I set up my moon altar. If I am working with fire then my moon altar has fire elements and I will use warm tones of yellow's, reds, oranges and many candles and shapes like pyramids. I have my choice of crystals that resonate with the fire element such as fire agate. I have my candle that represents my intentions and I place some crystals that I will be working with around my candle. Since I'm working with fire my candle should be red, yellow or orange.

Use a broom/wand to put protection around yourself and family

Take your wand, prayer stick, broom and point it to the east and begin to turn clockwise and pray:

In the east, south, west and north
A perfect circle casts love and hope
A perfect circle casts out fear and pain
We gather here tonight to raise the vibration of positivity and power
Come all, you are invited to this sacred space.
We have come here to celebrate the new moon.

Then everyone holds their broom or each other's hands and walks three times clockwise in a circle this signifies turning the yearly wheel.

Suggested chant: Spiral Chant or Cherokee Morning Chant

Stop here while the Circle Keeper says a prayer:

We ask for the God and Goddess's blessings over this gathering

(Face east): *Great Spirit of Light place of the rising sun*
Let there be light on our paths, let our fire always burn brightly with love and compassion. We thank you for the gift of fire.

(Face south): *Great Spirit of Love; fill our cups with your sacred waters. We thank you for water, it is the lifeblood of Mother Earth and it sustains our lives and all life on this planet. We thank you for the gift of water.*

(Face west): *Great Spirit of Life; thank you for our bodies thank you for our paths, never let us forget our connection to Mother Earth and our connection to spirit. Thank you for the gift of earth.*

(Face north): Thank you Great Spirit for the Creation of the universe and souls. Thank you for the air we breathe, thank you for the winds of creation — the four winds from the four kingdoms. Thank you for the messages they bring to us. We thank you for the gift of air.

May the gifts of nature and blessings of the wise sustain us this night and throughout our lives.

I lay out my healing crystals and then I smudge my crystals and myself. I ask the Creator to release the healing abilities of the crystals and to guide me to the crystal and element that wishes to work with me during this moon cycle.

Select crystals and charge them with protecting yourself and family. This is done by holding a crystal in both hands and praying that the Creator and Mother Earth will infuse the rose quartz (or whatever crystal you are using) with the ability to heal her heart.

If you are programming a crystal for protection, hold it to your heart or to your forehead and ask the Mother Earth and the Creator to awaken the protective powers within the crystal.

After you have programmed your crystals sit in a quiet meditative state and imagine a beautiful ball of white light encasing your stones, and then let it encase yourself and your area. You are creating a bubble of healing and protective energies around yourself and your items. Hold your crystal and ask what does this stone want to do for you? How would it like to help you and your family? Perhaps this crystal is more suited to grounding than uplifting so ask before you program.

The most important question you'll ask the stones is, will you work with me? Be accepting of the answer. Program some of your stones to be offering stones for when you are out in nature and would like to take something from the earth. When you take something such a branch, you can leave a crystal.

Finish the ritual with drumming and chanting.

Chapter Six

The Celtic Year and the Elements Earth Wheel

There are many of us who have a deep spirituality for the earth, and me, a deep spirituality centered around nature. I like to observe the changing of the seasons and perform a special ritual on the solstices and equinoxes.

Many cultures for thousands of years back to Neolithic people acknowledged events in nature such as the seasons changing. Perhaps it is ingrained somewhere within us to perform rituals that are connected to the earth. There are many types of pagans today and all pagans don't celebrate the same holidays, but the eight Sabbats are a beautiful model to practice by for anyone who wants to follow the natural cycles of the year.

One of the beautiful themes of pagan wisdom is working with the elements. Creating that balance within us is so important to our health, meditating on all the elements is our first step to learning more about the elements that are within us and around us.

The Elements Earth Wheel
The World is Within Me

The herbs that I use in this ceremony are cedar or rosemary and sometimes I will use a mixture of cedar and lavender but you can use whatever you like. The smoke from these blends is very earthy but also very uplifting. In each direction, an herb will be offered.

Just as the earthworm outside our window creeps and squirms around in the dirt and is part of the natural world so are we part of this mass ecosystem and so let's rejoice to our connection to earth and spirit. The elements of water, earth, fire, air and the fifth is spirit will be honored and tapped into during this ritual.

These elements are within us, they sustain us, the electrical impulses that fire in our brain are also in the fires that cook our foods and warm our homes. We have the element of water within us and we need water to drink, our food comes from the earth, and we need air to breath. We know this but we don't really feel this, in the Fivefold Elements Earth Wheel we connect with these elements and we connect with the Great Spirit.

I present Celtic themes here because the beauty of the symbol captured my creative spiritual self.

I prepare my altar with five small bowls each one has an element within it, for instance the air bowl has a feather. I have my cauldron or smudge pot and my herbs or resins. If you have a problem with smoke use an essential oil burner and add just a drop of oil to each direction. Smudge the ceremonial area, smudge yourself and others then offer smudge smoke to the seven directions. At the opening of the circle, place two candles for everyone to pass through this symbolizes being cleansed and ready for ritual, (the candles at entrance should be blessed candles).

Before I begin, I make this gesture and affirmation. I take my prayer stick in my left hand and draw the Celtic cross starting above my head I point my broom/wand upward and whisper *The Divine Creator*. I bring my prayer stick to the ground and say *Mother Earth*. I then go to the left of my body holding my stick I say *Sacred Door Keepers*. I bring my stick to the right of me and say *Sacred Earth Teachers*. Lastly, I make a circle and say *Sacred Circle of Life*. I lay my prayer stick down on a cloth and take another deep breath and stretch my arms out to form a cross. I say this prayer:

I stand, in the center of this sacred circle with arms outstretched in a pose of gratitude. I arise today through the power of the Creation that supports me, blesses me and heals me. I give thanks for my life and for nature and I humbly ask for Divine guidance in my life. May there be beauty above me, beauty within me and beauty below me.

The Elements Earth Wheel starts within the circle. The symbol for this ceremony is the fivefold symbol. The inner ring represents the Great Mystery, the circle of life, Spirit — the sacred fire that is within you and me. After this, I like to sit and do some chanting and drumming.

The Center Circle is Spirit and I choose the color of indigo. Within my spirit bowl, I have a piece of bread. I use bread because in many cultures food has always played a significant role in worship. Hot Cross Buns originated from the pagan culture, the cross represented the four quarters of the moon. Therefore, it is an appropriate idea to use these in the ceremony.

I offer my rosemary to my smudge bowl and as the smoke rises upwards. I pray:

We/I raise our hands to the Great Spirit, whose voice we hear in the wind, whose warmth we feel in the flames of the fire. I walk with reverence upon Mother Earth aware of her strength and beauty. I will take moments to feel the great power of nature. I want to meditate on the wonder of this world and to feel the Great Mystery in the waves of the oceans, life in one raindrop.

Creator we give you praise and thanks for your gift of life and for Mother Earth who sustains our lives and heals our bodies, we honor the Creator we honor all the elements.

I light my candle and pray:

I light this candle for spirit for I am love and light. I am an eternal being I came from love, I am love, and I send forth love.

Next, I take up my bread and I pray:

With this bread I celebrate and pay homage to the Great Spirit that I am part of and who is the author of all the elements, I ask for healing to occur within me and within this world.

Now we focus on the second ring

The Eastern Circle is the second ring and is the element of Air. Air is intuitive and psychic. The direction here is east. The color here is yellow. I light my candle that represents air and say this simple affirmation:

Integrity is the virtue of this element and direction, I will be honest with myself and my honestly with others will be molded from love.

I take my feather if I am working alone. If in a group, I will take a piece of parsley and eat the herb. Parsley is one of the foods that resonate with the element of air.

East and sunrise is a chance to start afresh each day. Breathe; our breathing keeps us alive. This simple unconscious act of taking in air is what keeps us on this earth plane. Imagine what it feels like to be a bird to soar on the winds high above the earth, total freedom. The exhilaration of flight and the feeling of wind illustrate how powerful the element of air is. Air can be turbulent like when a change or weather is coming or a storm and sometimes it's a gentle breeze cooling us off. Aim to be free, unleash the shackles in your life and follow your dreams and passions.

Offer your herbs to your smudge bowl and pray:

We/l raise our hands to the Great Spirit, whose voice we hear in the wind, whose warmth we feel in the flames of the fire. I walk with reverence upon Mother Earth aware of her strength and beauty. I will take moments to feel the great power of nature. I want to meditate on the wonder of this world and to feel the Great Mystery in the waves of the oceans, life in one raindrop.

Creator we give you praise and thanks for your gift of life and for Mother Earth who sustains our lives and heals our bodies, we honor the Creator we honor all the elements.

The Southern Circle is the third ring representing fire. The circle color here is red. Fire brings people together. The fire pit has long been regarded as a sacred spot where food was prepared and rituals were done.

Fire brings transformation. Fire is positive, it is expansion and it is masculine. If we need to make personal changes in our lives, this requires personal power and accessing the fire energy can enable us to bring about those transformations.

I light my candle for fire and visualize the flames of a bonfire and I smell the campfire smoke. When I hear the crackling sounds of the logs I allow its warmth to take me back in time to another lifetime. I am quiet within myself I acknowledge that I am an ancient being, the Kingdom of Creation is within me. I have lived many lifetimes, I have won and lost many battles, I am my memories and I am unique.

What battles are going on in your life? Are you winning or losing those battles? Have you chosen your weapons wisely? Who or what is your enemy and who or what are your allies?

My affirmation with my candle is as follows:

My thoughts that I think and the words that I speak are what creates my reality, I have the power to create a beautiful life.

If in a group, you can all take some cinnamon or pepper from the element bowl to help connect you with the energy of fire.

After this, I offer my herbs to my smudge bowl or cauldron and as the smoke rises, I say this prayer:

We/I raise our hands to the Great Spirit, whose voice we hear in the wind, whose warmth we feel in the flames of the fire. I walk with reverence upon Mother Earth aware of her strength and beauty. I will take moments to feel the great power of nature. I want to meditate on the wonder of this world and to feel the Great Mystery in the waves of the oceans, life in one raindrop.

Creator we give you praise and thanks for your gift of life and for Mother Earth who sustains our lives and heals our bodies, we honor the Creator we honor all the elements.

The Western Circle is the fourth ring means water. Water symbolizes Emotion. The color here is blue. I thank the Creator for water. Water soothes, cleanses, and clears away, refreshes, without water no life would exist. Water is healing especially our emotions. Intention is like a force in nature. Where our intention is that is where our energies are being aimed. What is your intention? Is it letting go of pain? Is it bringing a soul mate into your life or healing your body?

Light your candle for this element and say this simple affirmation:

Water heals me, water cleanses me and water calms me. I am fluid, I am flowing. My intention is to be more like water and move over and around the obstacles in my path.

Visualize staring at a beautiful lake on a sunny day, the water shimmers under the sunlight, throw a pebble into the water and watch as the ripples of water travel across the surface of the water. Be like these ripples of water and allow your intentions to spread outward in your life bring you a harvest of health and happiness. If you are in a group maybe have some rosehip tea because rosehips resonates with water.

Offer your herb to your smudge bowl and pray:

We/I raise our hands to the Great Spirit, whose voice we hear in the wind, whose warmth we feel in the flames of the fire. I walk with reverence upon Mother Earth aware of her strength and beauty. I will take moments to feel the great power of nature. I want to meditate on the wonder of this world and to feel the Great Mystery in the waves of the oceans, life in one raindrop.

Creator we give you praise and thanks for your gift of life and for Mother Earth who sustains our lives and heals our bodies, we honor the Creator we honor all the elements.

The Northern Circle is the fifth ring and is earth. The color here is green. Earth is our reality. Earth this is where material things grow, it is soil, it is mountains, it is the vast expanse of desert, it is so many beautiful and powerful things, but most importantly is it our home it is our mother. We need to cherish this earth and its resources and all living creatures within it. I light my candle and I give thanks to the Creator for my earthly home. My affirmation is:

I can create the life of my dreams, prosperity and abundance is flowing into all areas of my life.

The earth element is abundance and wealth. Holding my candle, I want to be aware that I am part of this incredible ecosystem. If you are in a group, you can eat some foods that resonate with the earth element such as liquorice or blueberries.

Then I offer my herbs to the smudge bowl and pray:

We/I raise our hands to the Great Spirit, whose voice we hear in the wind, whose warmth we feel in the flames of the fire. I walk with reverence upon Mother Earth aware of her strength and beauty. I will take moments to feel the great power of nature. I want to meditate on the wonder of this world and to feel the Great Mystery in the waves of the oceans, life in one raindrop.

Creator we give you praise and thanks for your gift of life and for Mother Earth who sustains our lives and heals our bodies, we honor the Creator we honor all the elements.

You can have a collection of items on your altar that represent all the elements and hold them or touch them during the ritual, of if in a group have them displayed so afterwards people can touch them this is suppose to be a tactile ritual.

We need moments of solitude and reflection to balance out how much we give and how much we keep for ourselves.

Use the Mother Earth Chant. Other chants that can be used are the Spiral Chant and Earth is Our Mother Chant.

The Celtic New Year

To begin our journey around the wheel of the year let us start with Samhain October 31st, which is the last harvest festival of the year and the Celtic New Year.

The year is dying, Samhain is one of the two doorways of the year the other being Beltane. The Celts divided the year into two seasons the light and the dark. Samhain literary means summers end.

Samhain to me is a magical time to communicate with the spirit world, to pray for those that have passed before us, to release baggage in my life and to understand that in darkness comes messages of hope. In my Earth Wheel Samhain, I practice some self-healing as well as appreciating the cycle of the year.

Yule/Winter Solstice is around December 21st. Here in the Northern Hemisphere the nights grow longer and the days grow shorter that is until the Winter Solstice then it begins to reverse. Yule comes from a Norse word and it means wheel, doesn't that make you want to think of a wheel of light glowing in a winter's darkness? And so within the Earth Wheel I celebrate the light and walk for healing of the planet.

Next on our journey is Imbolc and already into February this belongs to Brigit a Celtic Goddess. February 1st was known as the Feast of Lights, Feast of the Virgin and many more names. Imbolc or Oimelc these two names refer to the lactation of the ewes, the flow of milk. In the Earth Wheel Imbolc is all about the divine fire that glows at the center of the wheel, it is our divine fire that is inside of me and you.

The Spring Equinox or Ostara is around March 21st, this is when spring returns and it is the light half of the year when the days grow longer and warmer. In the Earth Wheel, I like to pay homage to my Earth Teachers and bless all my new seeds.

Beltane officially begins on moonrise of April 30th. In the Earth Wheel, l like to perform my ceremony at night and take a lesson from my moon teachings. Remembering that this is a spring moon, I take time to honor my spirit and this involves spiritual connections like soul mates and twin flames. Flowers are so important in this ritual and so I celebrate the beauty and wisdom of them.

The Summer Solstice is all about growth and expansion and this is the longest day of the year around June 21st. The beauty of life is everywhere. I celebrate the elements and focus my thoughts on how important the elements are to us and how important they are in ceremony.

Next is Lammas, which falls on August 1st. It is the first harvest so this is all about breads, grains and being grateful for the harvests in our lives. In the Earth Wheel, I feel this is a time of farewells and regrets so I want to tie up all those loose ends and say bye to things that hinder me.

The Autumn Equinox is around September 21st and also called Mabon. This is the completion of the harvest. It is a journey of death and eventual renewal, which will come in the spring. We focus upon a balance of light and dark and acknowledge them both in nature and in ourselves. One tip that I use if my rituals are to be held indoors is that instead of having a fire for the circle to focus on during chanting, I will have a circular canvas. This is lit with battery powered mini lights (wrapped inside the canvas), which gives the appearance of an illuminated disk painted in scenes of nature or elements the choice is yours.

(The first ceremony is usually what we enjoy with family and friends the second is generally my own private ritual. I have tried to adapt it to suit more than one participant.)

Samhain/ Halloween Ritual

Samhain or Halloween is a witch's favorite Sabbat or holiday. This is a pagans New Year a very powerful time to make contact with the dead to hear messages from our Ancestors and to perform divination. You don't have to be a witch to enjoy this special time of year. We remember the anticipation of trick and treating as a child and we watch our own little ones enjoy the holiday. This can leave us feeling let down that there is nothing for us adults to do other then dress up and head to the local bar or dance. If you would like to do a (dare I say it) ...ritual, then read on because this ritual is fun and yet it has spiritual meaning behind it. So invite your friends. Practice some divination after ceremony using cards, dice or even perhaps a crystal ball and enjoy a holiday feast. Thank you coming on this journey with me through the wheel of the year. Happy Samhain!

Items you will need for ceremony

Brooms or cords that people can hang onto to turn the wheel
Candles and matches
Samhain cookies, which are messages taped inside a paper
Divination cards such as tarot or an oracle deck of your choice
Colored paper in Halloween colors

Reflections before the ritual

The harvest is in; the mums are in full bloom and its pumpkin time again. The Halloween decorations are up and there is an expectation of fun and treats. We love to see the children so happy about getting dressed up but there is another side to this holiday; the spiritual side, the adult side. On October nights while walking, we gaze up at the harvest moon and we feel that ancient tug, that primitive yearning to dance and make magick. We humans sense that a powerful time is approaching and so it is. Remember this is a witch's New Year and so a new cycle begins in the Celtic Wheel of the Year, how have we changed? What seeds have we sown throughout the year and what will we harvest from them?

The veil between the worlds is at its thinnest. It is a time to speak to the dead and to receive messages from our Ancestors through divination. The spirit world is among us; let us celebrate this reunion with a sense of fun but also with reverence.

The purpose of the ceremony is to turn the wheel of the year by performing chanting and walking clockwise around the circle.

You will receive messages from the spirit world through the Samhain or Halloween cookies. To make these you will write down messages onto paper such as; *we determine our destination, choose the road of happiness or start each day with a grateful heart.* For inspiration look at websites or books with positive or spiritual affirmations and write them down within your paper cookies.

Ask the Divine to guide you in your Samhain messages.

For the selecting of cards, use tarot or oracle cards and have fun interpreting them for each other.

In all the rituals in this book, and just as a reminder, you will usually have an entrance to a circle. The circle is where people will gather around and perform the activities of the ceremony. The entrance to the circle should be marked by a table on each side. On this table, you can have some holy water in a dish. You can have some crystals that you have prayed over and programmed to keep all evil and negativity out. Catholic medals are also fine and you can have statues of angels or saints.

Place items that resonate with your spiritual beliefs and what you feel protects you. The alternative is having two good size candles that you have prayed over and perhaps anointed with some holy oil or olive oil, or poles in the ground decorated with feathers this will give the space a more native feeling.

The area of the ceremony is blessed with prayers and smudging. The two altars at the sides of the entrance of the circle are set up and blessed.

Everyone is smudged before entering the circle. Once everyone is inside the ceremonial area, there is an opening prayer and an invocation for protection for the circle.

Take your wand, prayer stick or broom and point it in the east and begin turning clockwise and pray:

In the east, south, west and north
A perfect circle casts love and hope
A perfect circle casts out fear and pain
We gather here tonight to raise the vibration of positivity and power
Come all, you are invited to this sacred space.
We have come here to celebrate Samhain

Then everyone holds their broom or each other's hands and walks three times clockwise in a circle this signifies turning the yearly wheel.

Suggested chant: Spiral Chant or Cherokee Morning Chant

Now stop while the Circle Keeper says a prayer:

We ask for the God and Goddess's blessings over this gathering

(Face east): *Great Spirit of Light place of the rising sun Let there be light on our paths, let our fire always burn brightly with love and compassion. We thank you for the gift of fire.*

(Face south): *Great Spirit of Love; fill our cups with your sacred waters. We thank you for water, it is the lifeblood of Mother Earth and it sustains our lives and all life on this planet. We thank you for the gift of water.*

(Face west): *Great Spirit of Life; thank you for our bodies thank you for our paths, never let us forget our connection to Mother Earth and our connection to spirit. Thank you for the gift of earth.*

(Face north): *Thank you Great Spirit for the Creation of the universe and souls. Thank you for the air we breathe, thank you for the winds of creation — the four winds from the four kingdoms. Thank you for the messages they bring to us. We thank you for the gift of air.*

May the gifts of nature and blessings of the wise sustain us this night and throughout our lives.

Then everyone holds their broom or each other's hands and walks three times clockwise in a circle this signifies turning the yearly wheel along with singing:

Winter, spring, summer, fall

We turn the wheel for the benefit of all
Winter, spring, summer, fall
We turn the wheel for ceremony calls.

Or any chant. Mother Earth or the Spiral Chant is fine.

Opening invocation — Circle Keeper says:

I honor and greet you all, welcome to our circle.

Say an opening prayer.

Candle is now lit for the Ancestors with this prayer:

The wheel of the year is turning and we find ourselves together on this Samhain eve. The veil is thin, our ancestors hear us, and they stand with us this night. Now when the grasses are dying and the leaves have turned we feel the ancient timeless beauty of the earth, we feel the night stretching back thousands of years. Ancient bonfires, ancient rituals bind us all together on this eve. Samhain the thin veil opens, messages sent and are received pray they will bode well.

Following this there is ritual dancing and drumming which means moving around the circle chanting one of the chants mentioned above as this brings up the energy of the circle.

The Circle Keeper holds a plate of Samhain cookies up to the sky and prays over them and then each person is called to come forward and receive their Samhain message from the ancestors.

The message received they can keep it or burn it in the cauldron.

While the messages are burned in a cauldron, everyone is silent until everyone is done. This is followed by chanting and turning the wheel with everyone holding their brooms or cords and moving clockwise.

The Circle Keeper gathers her cards and moves around the circle. The Keeper will stop randomly in front of a person and that person will select two cards one for themselves and one for someone else in the circle. Each person selects someone and hands them a card. This way everyone will end up with two cards

This little verse is what the Keeper of the Circle will say to a person:

Draw from me two cards that will be true
One for you and one for another

Then more dancing follows, chant or turn the wheel using cords or brooms.

Everyone stops. The Circle Keeper bows to everyone and everyone bows to the Circle Keeper and to others and affirms:

May the Goddess and God within me, honor the Goddess and God within you.

Everyone exits through the blessed gates.

Afterwards have a Samhain feast and everyone can share the meanings of the cards with each other.

Solitary or Group Samhain Ritual

Samhain ritual is about releasing the old and bringing in the new.

Prepare your Samhain altar with items that reflect the meanings of the festival, such as corn, Jack o' lanterns, colors of orange and black, grains and anything else you may wish to have. There should also be representations of the four elements.

Before I begin, I make this gesture and affirmation. I take my prayer stick in my left hand and draw the Celtic cross starting above my head I point my broom/wand upward and whisper The Divine Creator. I bring my prayer stick to the ground and say Mother Earth. I then go to the left of my body holding my stick I say Sacred Door Keepers. I bring my stick to the right of me and say Sacred Earth Teachers. Lastly, I make a circle and say Sacred Circle of Life. I lay my prayer stick down on a cloth and take another deep breath and stretch my arms out to form a cross. I say this prayer:

> *I stand, in the center of this sacred circle with arms outstretched in a pose of gratitude. I arise today through the power of the Creation that supports me, blesses me and heals me. I give thanks for my life and for nature and I humbly ask for Divine guidance in my life. May there be beauty above me, beauty within me and beauty below me.*

Write down what you want to release onto cornhusks or paper, preferably organic. If you are not burning any items then after the ritual bury these writings, or offer them to a river. Make a Samhain prayer stick and smudge it then hang it somewhere for protection and blessing, it is also a lovely idea to give these as gifts.

In the cauldron or smudge bowl, have perhaps copal resin or your favorite herb such as sage or sweet grass.

The center candle is the Samhain candle (instead of having a tree I have my candle within a Jack o' lantern) surrounded by four orange mini candles each pointing in a cardinal direction, east, south, west and north. Surround them all with thirteen grandmother moon candles I prefer using white mini candles or battery operated mini candles.

Once everything is ready, light all your candles starting with the Samhain candle and affirm a statement of gratitude for your ancestors for without them you would not be alive. Thank Creation for her beauty and her abundance.

If you are using a cauldron then I'd place it off to the side of your circle, if you are using a smudge bowl do the same.

With your ceremonial feather smudge the area, and yourself then offer smudge to the seven directions which is Upward to the Goddess/God or Creator, Downward to Mother Earth, Center of wheel is Self, to the East is Spiritual, South is Emotional, West is Physical, and North is Mental. (I am using copal resin for this ceremony but you can use whatever resonates with yourself).

Following this part of the ceremony, select a card from an oracle deck and read your message from spirit. Set your card on your altar to remind you of your Samhain message written on the cornhusk or paper. Then I take a mixture of herbs and I sprinkle them over my paper and fold it together. While I do this, I pray for these things to be released into the night then I offer them to the fire or earth.

In your cup or chalice have some grape juice of wine and offer this drink to the Creator and drink for prosperity in the coming year.

Afterwards follow this up with drumming and chanting.

Finish with a prayer:

Our lives travel in a circle. To be human is to travel all the directions of the wheel. We need to grow spiritually, emotionally, physically and mentally.

I see a bonfire on an ancient hilltop with my ancestors gathered all around

Winter Solstice/Yule Ritual

Winter Solstice or Yule in pagan circles is a beautiful time of year being so close to Christmas it gives an extra festive feeling. If you have decided to have a winter solstice party this ritual is perfect. It is simple yet meaningful and easy to put together. After the ceremony, you can have a feast and you can perform some divination for each other using runes, cards whatever resonates with yourself. If you like you can use God and Goddess in your ritual or you can use Creator or even just Creation, the choice is yours depending on your spiritual path. Thank you for taking the journey with me and I send you tidings of peace and joy this Yuletide season.

What items you will need for this ceremony

Candles

Brooms or cords for turning the wheel

Herbs for smudging such as cedar or sweet pine

Tables

Yule or Christmas decorations

Bowl of water (for the Yule wishing well)

Wishing stones you can use river or store bought small crystals.

Items that represent all of the elements fire, water, earth and air

Reflections before ritual

Yule is the winter solstice the shortest day of the year, but the good news is that after this day our daylight hours become longer. The earth is in deep slumber now, but the solstice brings hope. Beautifully, serenely, in the quietness of winter's chill the sun is reborn. The promise of the warmth returning has been fulfilled again. From this day forward as the wheel turns towards Imbolc the warmth and the light grows stronger.

But let us remain in this moment of magic for even in our

darkest hour the light is our promise; the promise of hope and love. We are now in the season of goodwill and friendship. Messages of faith and trust abound and bring us out of the dark. This is the season of giving, and in performing this ceremony, you will give others the chance to bring their own miracles of healing and peace. This ritual is about bringing light to the darkness.

The purpose of this ceremony is to bring light and to give thanks and to make wishes for a prosperous future. You will need a center table decorated with items for winter and Christmas if you like. A bowl of water that will be used to place your stones in, and people will make a wish as they offer their stones to this wishing well. You can use a pail decorated up for Yule, use your imagination and have fun with it. On the center table there should be a Yule Candle smudging herbs and a smudge bowl, stones for the wishes, these stones need to be cleansed by smudging them and washing them. You can decorate them if you chose.

You will need four tables facing east, south, west and north and you can decorate the tables in a winter festive fashion.

The Circle Keeper will call people to come forward to the center table and with their candle lit they will carry it to the east, they will say a simple affirmation which will be told to them when they come up for their candle. Each person will carry a candle to the four directions bringing messages of joy and peace to the solstice evening. Then as a closing fun activity everyone can approach the center altar and offer a stone to the wishing well and make a wish.

The ritual begins with smudging people, area and smudging the two tables that stand on either side of the entrance of your circle. On your entrance altars you can have blessed items displayed and pray that no evil can pass through these blessed tables.

After the smudging and prayer gates are blessed and people

enter circle.

At beginning of the ritual, we need to cast our circle of protection light one pillar candle at center table where the bowl of water sits and pray

Take your wand, prayer stick or broom and point it to the east and begin to turn clockwise and pray:

In the east, south, west and north
A perfect circle casts love and hope
A perfect circle casts out fear and pain
We gather here tonight to raise the vibration of positivity and power
Come all, you are invited to this sacred space.
We have come here to celebrate the Winter Solstice

Then everyone holds their broom or each other's hands and walks three times clockwise in a circle this signifies turning the yearly wheel.

Suggested chant: Spiral Chant or Cherokee Morning Chant.

Now stop while the Circle Keeper says a prayer:

We ask for the God and Goddess's blessings over this gathering

(Face east): *Great Spirit of Light place of the rising sun*
Let there be light on our paths, let our fire always burn brightly with love and compassion. We thank you for the gift of fire.

(Face south): *Great Spirit of Love; fill our cups with your sacred waters. We thank you for water, it is the lifeblood of Mother Earth and it sustains our lives and all life on this planet. We thank you for the gift of water.*

(Face west): *Great Spirit of Life; thank you for our bodies thank you for our paths, never let us forget our connection to Mother Earth*

and our connection to spirit. Thank you for the gift of earth.

(Face north): *Thank you Great Spirit for the Creation of the universe and souls. Thank you for the air we breathe, thank you for the winds of creation — the four winds from the four kingdoms. Thank you for the messages they bring to us. We thank you for the gift of air.*

May the gifts of nature and blessings of the wise sustain us this night and throughout our lives.

Chanting and singing follow for a while.

We hold brooms or we hold hands and turn the wheel and chant :

Blessings to you Heavenly Father, Blessings to you Earthly Mother.
Blessings to you Angels of winter and peace
I Bless myself, I honor myself, I respect myself, I love myself for who I am.

Opening prayer:

The chilling breath of winter is touching us
A time of the deepest darkness
And yet a spark of something bright touches us.
Could this be the dawning of the approaching light?
We lift our hands and call forth the light from the womb of the night.

The Circle Keeper calls the first person forward and hands them a candle, which they light from the Yule candle. She/he tells them to take it to the east where they light the east candle. While the person is doing this, the Circle Keeper proclaims that the candle is taken to the east:

...let our light guide us in the darkness.

The person leaves their candle and takes a seat and another person is called forth. The Circle Keeper hands them a candle, which they light from the Yule candle, and as the person takes the candle to the south where they will light another candle it is proclaimed:

...in the stillness of this sacred night let this light heal our painful memories.

The person leaves their candle there and return to their seat.

The Circle Keeper calls another person forward and hands them a candle. The person lights their candle from the Yule candle and walks to the west of the circle where on the table they light another candle. The Keeper of the Circle proclaims:

... we carry this light on this darkest night to bring hope to us and to the world.

The person leaves their candle there and returns to their seat.

The Keeper of the Circle calls another person to come and light a candle. This person lights their candle from the Yule candle and carries it to the north. The Keeper of the Circle proclaims:

The promise has been kept tonight the sun is reborn from this day forward the warmth and the sun shall grow stronger each day, the light will always return we will always have rebirth.

The person leaves their candle there and return to their seat.

The Circle Keeper with their Yule candle now walks around

the inside the circle and prays or affirms:

This light represents our intuitive light, seeking and acceptance in
perfect harmony, love and light in balance this night.

Dancing and the raising of the vibration of the circle follows. You
can chant the Mother Earth Chant or another chant of your
choice.

The Circle Keeper offers something to the bowl of water as an
offering such as an herb or spice such as cinnamon and prays
that the Divine will grant the wishes of the people this night.
Now the Keeper calls everyone up to take a cleansed stone hold
it in their hands and make a wish and then offer the stone to the
wishing well.

Come stand at the bowls edge; hold it in your hands
Now cast it (wishing stone) *into the wishing bowl.*

Then everyone holds their broom or each other's hands and
walks three times clockwise in a circle. This signifies turning the
yearly wheel along with singing:

Winter, spring, summer, fall
We turn the wheel for the benefit of all
Winter, spring, summer, fall
We turn the wheel for ceremony calls.

Everyone stops. The Circle Keeper bows to everyone and
everyone bows to the Circle Keeper and to the others and
affirms:

May the Goddess and God within me, honor the Goddess and God
within you.

Everyone exits through the blessed gates.

After the ceremony, the stones are gathered and buried into the earth and prayed over:

We ask our earthly mother to take our wishes and let them come true if it is for the good of all.

Solitary or Group Winter Solstice Ritual

Darkest night tonight it will surely be.
Yule /Winter Solstice the wheel of the year continues to turn and now we land upon the winter solstice.

This is another ceremony, which I have performed at Yule, I hope you like it.

I like to have my altar set up for the Winter Solstice and decorate it with pinecones, evergreens, reds, greens, and many candles, colorful mini lights and have the elements represented in some fashion. Use your imagination and have fun.

It is a common misconception that all pagans worship trees. I do not but I do revere them, so for the Yule ritual I like to have a decorated potted evergreen in the center of the ritual area with lots of decorations. In the spring, I plant it outside. I like to have many lights in and around the ritual area, as this is a ritual where we are calling back the sun and appreciating the knowledge that the days are slowly growing longer. This time of year, I find myself in my northern quadrant of my Earth Wheel and I give thanks to my Earth Teachers. The element that I revere here is also acknowledged and both are somehow displayed on my altar. I have pictures of creatures or herbs and the element of air with lots of feathers.

The ceremony begins with the smudging ceremony which involves smudging self or each other, smudging area and offering smudge smoke to the seven directions which is to the

God/Goddess or Creator, Mother Earth, Spirit, East, South, West and North.

Before I begin, I make this gesture and affirmation. I take my prayer stick in my left hand and draw the Celtic cross starting above my head I point my broom/wand upward and whisper *The Divine Creator*. I bring my prayer stick to the ground and say *Mother Earth*. I then go to the left of my body holding my stick I say *Sacred Door Keepers*. I bring my stick to the right of me and say *Sacred Earth Teachers*. Lastly, I make a circle and say *Sacred Circle of Life*. I lay my prayer stick down on a cloth and take another deep breath and stretch my arms out to form a cross. I say this prayer:

> *I stand, in the center of this sacred circle with arms outstretched in a pose of gratitude. I arise today through the power of the Creation that supports me, blesses me and heals me. I give thanks for my life and for nature and I humbly ask for Divine guidance in my life. May there be beauty above me, beauty within me and beauty below me.*

> *Night surrounds me I feel a chilling peacefulness*

I light my Yule candle then I pray or affirm a blessing such as:

> *This solstice flame burns bright for tonight; I celebrate the light returning to the earth. Grandfather sun you are the author of all sacred light, bless this new flame.*

> *I revel in the morning light gleaming across the land, bringing warmth and life back to Mother Earth. May my prayers shine into the spiritual realm like the sun glittering on the snow so that out of the darkness of winter my love can join with all light workers to shatter all darkness in this world and beyond. Bless my feet as I walk for peace, love and healing for all.*

I then light my first of my four cardinal candles starting in the northern direction, I ring my bell and say this prayer:

I pray that the winds of the north take my prayers to the Great Mystery and I pray for peace, healing and love to flow to all the eastern quarters of this world.

I do this in all of the four directions.

This is optional depending on if you regularly look to your Earth Teachers for guidance and wisdom through your year, as I do. This night is one on which I will sometimes ask for a new Teacher and bless and release former earth. However, always I acknowledge a sacred color and Earth Teacher when I pray in each direction.

I take my Yule candle and walk in a sacred circle (smudge feet or anoint feet with an oil before you walk). This circle is the hoop of life that connects us all. I pray as I walk. I prefer to keep my thoughts on being in a state of gratitude on the longest night of the year, appreciating how beautiful is night. This is when we rest from many of our outside activities. For us in Canada, it is when the colder weather drives us inside and this gives us an opportunity to spend time with our loved ones. Winter is a natural process in our natural world, animals hibernate, birds migrate and Mother Nature sleeps. This is a season for us to rest and retreat into the warmth of our burrows. Slowly my thoughts turn to the message of this season, peace on earth, goodwill towards men … I walk and pray for humanity and all creatures of this world.

When I have finished, I find my seat and do some drumming and chanting or singing.

A feast can follow or a delicious treat for yourself if you are alone but whatever you do not forget to feed Mother Earth by offering some food to her from your feast.

As we turn the wheel this night
We summon our healing light
To heal us on this moonlit night

Imbolc Ritual

Imbolc February 1st, beginning at sundown. Imbolc is the first of the three spring Sabbats for pagans. On the 1st February here in Canada we're still in the dark months of winter but we notice that the days are very so slowly getting longer. Some days you can even notice a bit more warmth from the sun.

If you have decided to have an Imbolc party or just a party to break up the dreariness of winter then this is ritual is perfect. It is simple yet meaningful and easy to put together. After the ceremony, you can have a feast and you can perform some divination for each other using runes, cards whatever resonates with yourself. If you wish, you can refer to the Triple Goddess known as Brigid or you can refer to her as Saint Brigit, you can use God and Goddess in your ritual or you can use Creator or even just Creation, the choice is yours depending on your spiritual path. Thank you for taking the journey with me Happy Imbolc.

What items you will need for this ceremony

Herbs to smudge with and a smudging bowl
Tables
Candles
Reflections before the ritual

Outside the circle fill with candles or electric candles, mini lights but it has to be a circle of light. We are rejoicing over the lengthening days and spring is coming.

The Circle Keeper will require an assistant.

Beginning of the Ceremony

The area of the ceremony is blessed with prayers and smudging. The two altars at the sides of the entrance of the circle are set up and blessed.

Everyone is smudged before entering the circle. Once everyone is inside the ceremonial area, there is an opening prayer and an invocation for protection for the circle.

Take your wand, prayer stick or broom and point it to the east and begin turning clockwise and pray:

In the east, south, west and north
A perfect circle casts love and hope
A perfect circle casts out fear and pain
We gather here tonight to raise the vibration of positivity and power
Come all, you are invited to this sacred space.
We have come here to celebrate Samhain

Suggested chant: Spiral Chant or Cherokee Morning Chant

Now stop while the Circle Keeper says a prayer:

We ask for the God and Goddess's blessings over this gathering

(Face east): *Great Spirit of Light place of the rising sun*
Let there be light on our paths, let our fire always burn brightly with love and compassion. We thank you for the gift of fire.

(Face south): *Great Spirit of Love; fill our cups with your sacred waters. We thank you for water, it is the lifeblood of Mother Earth and it sustains our lives and all life on this planet. We thank you for the gift of water.*

(Face west): *Great Spirit of Life; thank you for our bodies thank you for our paths, never let us forget our connection to Mother Earth* *and our connection to spirit. Thank you for the gift of earth.*

*(**Face north**): Thank you Great Spirit for the Creation of the universe and souls. Thank you for the air we breathe, thank you for the winds of creation — the four winds from the four kingdoms. Thank you for the messages they bring to us. We thank you for the gift of air.*

May the gifts of nature and blessings of the wise sustain us this night and throughout our lives.

Then everyone holds their broom or each other's hands and walks three times clockwise in a circle this signifies turning the yearly wheel along with singing:

Winter, spring, summer, fall
We turn the wheel for the benefit of all
Winter, spring, summer, fall
We turn the wheel for ceremony calls.

Everyone can sit down, the Circle Keeper lights three candles on the altar. These candles represent purification, awakening, Goddess Brighid or if you wish the third candle can represent dedication to goals and spiritual growth.

In honor of the healing waters of Saint Brighid we will pray to her to bless our water and afterwards we will all drink it.

The Circle Keeper prays over the water:

Saint/Goddess Brigid bless these waters with your holiness and purity. Help us to see the world with fresh eyes and a world of endless possibilities for us to grow and learn.

You can use your chalice if you have one or a glass and call people to come forward and drink from the water.

We sit and meditate for a few moments; someone can drum if they wish.

The assistant walks around and hands to each person a small mini candle and lights it, when the circle is complete and everyone has a lit candle in front of them, the Circle Keeper prays:

Sacred fire burn bright
Heal us on this special night
Burn for Brigid, for Brigid Bright!

We walk three times around the circle (with our candles) for purification our lives.

I offer this flame to Brigid Bright.

Everyone blows out their candles at the same time.

Closing chant:

Night of the white candles
The darkness turned into light
Flames lit for Brigid purify us this night

Solitary or Group Imbolc Ritual

Imbolc is known as a festival of fire

Everything is new at Imbolc. On this first of the spring Sabbats, early February may seem like a dreary time of year with all the snow and slush but what a perfect time to have a ritual of lights, colors and crystals. Candlemas is the Christianized name for the holiday another name is Brigid's Day in honor of the Celtic Goddess Brigid.

This Sabbat for me is a time for me to honor the light that is within us all, the light of the Divine.

I take the time now to bless my candles and my crystals and to reconnect with my sacred colors. My ceremony is about fire, light, crystals and colors and so my altar has many different colors. My candles are all colors too and surrounded by beautiful crystals. I have my Imbolc candle surrounded by my four candles facing the four cardinal directions and a circle of thirteen moon candles. I also have any candles or crystals that I need to bless. I start by smudging my area, then myself and then offer smudge smoke to the seven directions as with previous rituals.

Before I begin, I make this gesture and affirmation. I take my prayer stick in my left hand and draw the Celtic cross starting above my head I point my broom/wand upward and whisper *The Divine Creator*. I bring my prayer stick to the ground and say *Mother Earth*. I then go to the left of my body holding my stick I say *Sacred Door Keepers*. I bring my stick to the right of me and say *Sacred Earth Teachers*. Lastly, I make a circle and say *Sacred Circle of Life*. I lay my prayer stick down on a cloth and take another deep breath and stretch my arms out to form a cross. I say this prayer:

> *I stand, in the center of this sacred circle with arms outstretched in a pose of gratitude. I arise today through the power of the Creation that supports me, blesses me and heals me. I give thanks for my life and for nature and I humbly ask for Divine guidance in my life. May there be beauty above me, beauty within me and beauty below me.*

I light my Imbolc candle first and then proceed to light the rest of my candles. I bring my crystal to my heart and I say a prayer and bless myself. I bless my spirit and my life and promise myself that I will nurture others and myself. My spirit is my sacred fire my Imbolc candle represents my sacred fire.

I pass my crystals through the smudge smoke saying a prayer of blessing over my stones. I then take my ceremonial candles, anoint them with oil and bless them saying prayers over them; then I proceed to work with my colors. I hold my glass of colored water with the floating candle and I absorb that color into me. I tune into this color and feel what its vibration feels like, how does this color effect me? Then I picture myself encased in the color at which I am gazing. I do this with all the colors I work with during this ritual.

I raise my hands and say a prayer of blessing for humankind and my loved ones that the light of the divine engulfs every-where and everyone. Then I offer an herb to the smudge bowl and give thanks. In honor to the Triple Goddess or the Holy Trinity, I honor my "tripleness" that is my soul, mind and body. I light three candles (which I have anointed with oil) for spirit, mind and body. After lighting these candles I pray:

With my spirit, I connect with the Divine, with my mind I send out positive thoughts and intentions and with my body, I promise myself to be faithful to the path of peace and compassion.

I offer up smoke for my body and make an affirmation to take care of my body, then I offer up smudge smoke to honor my mind and add smudge to honor my spirit. I follow this with drumming and chanting before closing the ceremony.

Spring Equinox Ritual/Ostara

Spring equinox or Ostara in pagan circles; whatever you chose to call it, is a beautiful time of year. New growth and the antici-pation of warmer weather make us very happy. If you have decided to have spring equinox party and you love herbs and would like to learn how to use them then this ritual is perfect, it is simple yet meaningful and easy to put together. After the ceremony, you can have a feast, and drink some herbal teas. As with the other rituals, you can perform some divination for each other using oracle cards. You can also have herbs or flowers as part of the ceremony. If you wish, you can use the God and Goddess in your ritual, or you can use Creator or even just Creation, the choice is yours depending on your spiritual path. Thank you for taking the journey with me, and have a blessed Spring Equinox.

What items you will need for this ceremony
Bowls
Herbs
Candles
Herbs for smudging

Reflections before ceremony
Spring equinox is a day when there are equal amounts of daylight and equal amounts of darkness. With the balance of day and night we seek balance in our own lives of working and rest.

Depending on where you live, you will have snow or already plants will be growing. Being aware of the seasons and how nature and herbs sustain our lives and enrich our lives is essential to having earth-based spirituality. Nature is our way of life, and what a perfect balance that life should be. We look around and see life returning, the days are growing warmer and longer. A part of the magic of Mother Earth is in her herbs and flowers we ask for healthy gardens this season. Spring brings change there is newness and the wonder of life.

To begin, the area of the ceremony is blessed with prayers and smudging. The two altars at the sides of the entrance of the circle are set up and blessed.

Everyone is smudged before entering the circle. Once

everyone is inside the ceremonial area, there is an opening prayer and an invocation for protection for the circle.

Take your wand, prayer stick or broom, point it to the east and begin turning clockwise and pray:

In the east, south, west and north
A perfect circle casts love and hope
A perfect circle casts out fear and pain
We gather here tonight to raise the vibration of positivity and power
Come all, you are invited to this sacred space.
To celebrate Ostara the Spring Equinox time.

Suggested chant: Spiral Chant or Cherokee Morning Chant

Then everyone holds their broom or each other's hands and walks three times clockwise in a circle this signifies turning the yearly wheel.

Winter, spring, summer, fall
We turn the wheel for the benefit of all
Winter, spring, summer, fall
We turn the wheel for ceremony calls.

Now stop while the Circle Keeper says a prayer:

We ask for the God and Goddess's blessings over this gathering

(Face east): *Great Spirit of Light place of the rising sun*
Let there be light on our paths, let our fire always burn brightly with love and compassion. We thank you for the gift of fire.

(Face south): *Great Spirit of Love; fill our cups with your sacred waters. We thank you for water, it is the lifeblood of Mother Earth and it sustains our lives and all life on this planet. We thank you for* *the gift of water.*

(Face west): *Great Spirit of Life; thank you for our bodies thank you for our paths, never let us forget our connection to Mother Earth and our connection to spirit. Thank you for the gift of earth.*

(Face north): *Thank you Great Spirit for the Creation of the universe and souls. Thank you for the air we breathe, thank you for the winds of creation — the four winds from the four kingdoms. Thank you for the messages they bring to us. We thank you for the gift of air.*

May the gifts of nature and blessings of the wise sustain us this night and throughout our lives.

Take any herbs and/or flowers to the east. Place on the table facing east within the circle and pray:

The spirits of the plants heal our spirits they take our prayers to the Creator. Their fragrance is soothing to the God and Goddess they pray on our behalf, we thank them and honor them for their gift as spirit helpers.

Now we take our bowl of herbs and/or flowers to the southern table, we place our bowl there and pray:

We give thanks for the spirit of the plants ability to heal our emotions to balance our feelings to bring clarity and hope to us. We thank them for helping us with our emotions.

Now we take our bowl of herbs and or flowers to the western part of the circle, place it down, and give thanks for the healing power of herbs over our physical ailments by praying:

We give thanks for healing cancer, arthritis and all diseases. We honor their ability to bring health to our bodies.

Now we take a bowl of herbs and or flowers to the northern section of our circle and place it down and give thanks for the herbs that heal our minds:

We give thanks for the herbs that drive away depression, insomnia, fear we thank them for soothing our worries and helping our brains and our thoughts.

The Circle Keeper lights the spring solstice candle and carries it around the circle giving a blessing of light and hope.

The celebration of Ostara is here, the spring equinox, raise your cups to cheer for spring, warm days ahead, sunshine to soothe our bodies and help our souls!

The Circle Keeper bows to everyone and everyone bows to the Circle Keeper and to others and affirms:

May the Goddess and God within me, honor the Goddess and God within you.

Everyone exits through the blessed gates.

Solitary or Group Spring Equinox Ritual

The World is within me

At the changing of the seasons, I like to break down my Earth Wheel and show gratitude to the elements and Earth Teachers within my sacred hoop.

During this powerful time is an excellent occasion for giving thanks and releasing the Earth Teachers who have taught me many lessons. I prepare to ask new ones that wish to come forward and help me on my spiritual journey. Stones that have been used to represent Earth Teachers can be buried or offered to a river or fire. It is with much appreciation that we say goodbye and perhaps they will come forward to help us again.

So, in preparation of the equinox I am busy painting or making new items that will represent my new Earth Teachers. Sometimes I make prayer sticks to represent Earth Teachers.

In the days or weeks, leading up to the equinox I will do meditations and reflections of elements, objects or creatures that I desire to work with and hopefully some will come forward to me.

Prepare your spring altar incorporating all the elements into it such as fire, water, earth and air. Smudge yourself and if you are not alone smudge the others then fan your smoke to the seven directions.

Before I begin, I make this gesture and affirmation. I take my prayer stick in my left hand and draw the Celtic cross starting above my head I point my broom/wand upward and whisper *The Divine Creator*. I bring my prayer stick to the ground and say *Mother Earth*. I then go to the left of my body holding my stick I say *Sacred Door Keepers*. I bring my stick to the right of me and say *Sacred Earth Teachers*. Lastly, I make a circle and say *Sacred Circle of Life*. I lay my prayer stick down on a cloth and take another deep breath and stretch my arms out to form a cross. I say this prayer:

> *I stand, in the center of this sacred circle with arms outstretched in a pose of gratitude. I arise today through the power of the Creation that supports me, blesses me and heals me. I give thanks for my life and for nature and I humbly ask for Divine guidance in my life. May there be beauty above me, beauty within me and beauty below me.*

For this ritual, you will need five candles in all. The center candle represents the Creator or if you like Creation. Surround this center candle with four candles each pointing in the cardinal directions of east, south, west and north. Thirteen candles that represent the moons of creation surround this.

The candle pointing in the eastern direction is the cardinal candle and in my ritual, this means that the candle is representing my Earth Teachers and so on in each direction. You can decorate the Creator candle for the spring equinox or placed in a glass container that you can decorate with flowers and so forth. Beside your Earth Teacher candles, place your totem stick that represents an Earth Teacher that you have been working with or a former one that you are releasing.

Once everything has been set up and everything has been smudged, you can begin the ritual.

Facing east light your Creator candle in the center of the circle of candles and give thanks to the Creator/Creation for the four winds that bring us our seasons and for bringing us messages. Give thanks to Mother Earth for our food, medicine and home we hope our minds and hearts are one with nature.

Light the cardinal candle that is pointing to the eastern direction and give thanks to your custodian that is in the eastern quadrant of the wheel. Continue and give thanks in all four directions lighting the candles as you travel around your wheel.

After lighting the candles, light your smudging herbs and as the smoke rises upwards give thanks to the water that quenches our thirst; give thanks to the air we breathe; give thanks for the fire that keeps us warm; and give thanks for the plants that feed us.

Take some smoke and bring it to your heart, now your heart and mind are one with nature.

If you are seeking the fellowship of a new Earth Teacher then pick up the totem sticks that represent the Earth Teacher smudge the stick, hold the stick to your chest, and pray for a new Earth

Teacher. Alternatively, give thanks for the ones that you have and request that they continue to impart their wisdom with you. Over the coming months, it is wise to learn as much as you can about your Earth Teachers. As you study them, the Creator will reveal secrets about yourself to you, in order that you can grow spirituality. This ritual can be performed at every equinox and solstice.

I use this variation for the spring ritual. First, I perform a smudging ritual. I have my Earth Teacher stones displayed and my spring equinox tree on my altar, which is a sprig of cedar decorated with eggs, ribbons and so on. I also display my elements.

In this ritual, I am honoring the equal time of day and night, taking a moment to realize how important the wheel of the year is and how by being aware of it, keeps me attuned to the natural rhythms of the seasons. Light is so important to life on this planet and it is symbolic to the balance that must be maintained within myself. We are travelling into the light half of the year and so I wish to harness that light and keep it within myself. So this is somewhat like the autumn equinox but our focus in on the light we have of ourselves. What do we need to cultivate more? What do we offer to our families and communities? This is a ritual of appreciating the fact that we are light workers and we want to honor the light. In honor of my inner light, I perform a small active meditation that helps me focus. I light one black candle and one white candle.

I am traveling into the light part of the year, spring has arrived and it is a time of planting and growth. I chose to plant good seeds to tend — that which is the best in me. I harness my light and the light of the Goddess/God, Creator. I bless my seeds that I am going to plant and keep the color white around my pots to remind me that I am honoring that light inside of myself. I smudge my seeds and smudge my potting supplies asking for an excellent growing season and a bountiful harvest.

I close with chanting and drumming I prefer to chant The Earth is Our Mother Chant.

Beltane Ritual

Beltane is the last of the three spring fertility festivals, the others being Ostara and Imbolc. Beltane is also the second important festival the other being Samhain.

Celebrated approximately halfway between Vernal (spring) equinox and the midsummer (Summer Solstice). Beltane traditionally marked the arrival of summer in ancient times.

If you have decided to have a party for Beltane this ritual is perfect and is simple yet meaningful and easily put together. After the ceremony, you can have a feast, perform some divination for each other using runes, cards or whatever resonates with you. If you like, you can use the God and Goddess in your ritual or you can use the Creator or even just Creation, the choice is yours depending on your spiritual path. Thank you for taking the journey with me Happy Beltane.

What items you will need for this ceremony

Herbs to smudge with such as rosemary and sweet grass
Candles
Mini Maypoles
Water spray bottle with essential oil

Reflections before the ritual

Beltane is the light part of the year. Our ancestors divided the year into two parts, Samhain being the beginning of the dark part and Beltane being the beginning of the light part. Samhain is about honoring death and Beltane is about honoring life. It's a time when the sun is released from the chains of winter and is released. We welcome the longer days, the warmth of sunshine. We say that the veil between the living and the dead is thin at Samhain; this is also true at Beltane so this is an excellent time for divination and receiving messages from spirit.

Beltane translated means "fire of Bel" or "bright fire" — the "bale-fire". The Maypole is an important element to Beltane festivities, it is a tall pole decorated with long brightly colored ribbons, leaves, flowers and wreaths. Young maidens and lads each hold the end of a ribbon, and dance revolving around the base of the pole, interweaving the ribbons. The circle of dancers should begin, as far out from the pole as the length of ribbon allows, so the ribbons are taut. There should be an even number of boys and girls. Boys should be facing clockwise and girls counter clockwise. They each move in the direction that they are facing, weaving with the next and around braiding the ribbons over, under and around the pole. Those passing on the inside will have to duck, those passing on the outside raise their ribbons to slide over those on the inside. As the dancers revolve around the pole, the ribbons will weave creating a pattern. It is said that the pattern will indicate the abundance of harvest year. In this ritual, we'll be doing a smaller version of the Maypole.

The purpose of this ceremony is to make a sacred time to honor ourselves and appreciate and take care of our energy fields — our auras. When our auras are clear and clean, the effects on our health are amazing. Negative people or situations won't be able to penetrate our energy fields. A dirty and weak aura lets in fear and hurt this can damage our health. Earth, air, water and fire are excellent purifiers. Walking in bare feet on green grass allows our auras to be cleansed and repaired as our energies go down into Mother Earth. Being out in the wind cleanses us as does water. Having a salt bath or a shower will whisk away negative energies we may have come in contact with during our day. Fire is the most effective purifier of all. Since Beltane is a fire ceremony I think we should focus on fire first as a cleanser than finish with water, it will give our energies a nice contrast of cleaning

The preparation for this ritual involves having two blessed

gates at the entry point of the circle. Like in the other rituals, these are small tables, which can hold blessed candles, blessed statues of angels and deities, cleansed crystals or whatever you choose to be a source of protection to keep unwanted negative energies out of your circle.

Your two altars that sit on either side of the entrance of your circle and your center altar should all have a theme of spring and spring tones of color.

Take your smudge stick and sweep the area moving clockwise and whilst praying. Do not forget to bless the tables at the entrance of the circle.

The host should call the people into the circle. Remember people should enter through the blessed gates.

Smudge everyone as they enter the circle. Once everyone is inside the ceremonial area, say an opening prayer and an invocation for protection for the circle.

Take your wand, prayer stick or broom and point it to the east and begin turning clockwise and pray:

In the east, south, west and north
A perfect circle casts love and hope
A perfect circle casts out fear and pain
We gather here tonight to raise the vibration of positivity and power
Come all, you are invited to this sacred space.
We have come here to celebrate Beltane

Then everyone holds their broom or each other's hands and walks three times clockwise in a circle this signifies turning the yearly wheel.

As we turn the wheel this night
We summon our healing light
To heal us on this sacred night.
We turn the wheel three times to achieve harmony within ourselves.

Or any chant like Mother Earth or Spiral Chant is fine.

Now stop while the Circle Keeper says a prayer:

We ask for the God and Goddess's blessings over this gathering

(Face east): *Great Spirit of Light place of the rising sun Let there be light on our paths, let our fire always burn brightly with love and compassion. We thank you for the gift of fire.*

(Face south): *Great Spirit of Love; fill our cups with your sacred waters. We thank you for water, it is the lifeblood of Mother Earth and it sustains our lives and all life on this planet. We thank you for the gift of water.*

(Face west): *Great Spirit of Life; thank you for our bodies thank you for our paths, never let us forget our connection to Mother Earth and our connection to spirit. Thank you for the gift of earth.*

(Face north): *Thank you Great Spirit for the Creation of the universe and souls. Thank you for the air we breathe, thank you for the winds of creation — the four winds from the four kingdoms. Thank you for the messages they bring to us. We thank you for the gift of air.*

May the gifts of nature and blessings of the wise sustain us this night and throughout our lives.

Opening invocation — Circle Keeper says:

I honor and greet you all, welcome to our circle.

On the center altar, we will light five candles:
The first candle is lit for Beltane as a candle of love and light

to bless this sacred circle. The second candle is lit to welcome the Beltane fire of desire to warm our lives. The third candle is lit for the winter chill that is leaving our land. The fourth candle is lit for purification. Finally, the fifth candle is lit for the Beltane dance.

It is Beltane time again, the first day of the light half of the Celtic year. The Beltane sacred flame will purify us tonight. This night we are cleansed by Fire. That which is below and within, meets with that which is above — joined together in love.

Everyone joins in, in the lighting of the path of purification. Once the circle of candles is lit the ritual of cleansing begins. The host or assistant stands at the entrance of the circle of light and says this affirmation with each person before they travel the circle.

As you travel this ceremonial path tonight, allow the Beltane candles restore you health and strength this night.

After everyone has traveled the path of candlelight, there will be chanting and drumming.

Finally, we will purify with water and as people finish walking the path of candlelight, allow them to stand in front of the Circle Keeper and then spray them with a mixture of water and sandalwood or water and lavender.

Do your research to see what oils are best. They can be put into in a spritzer, but be careful not to aim at the face. We wouldn't want anyone getting this spray in their eyes.

An herbal offering is made to the cauldron or smudge bowl for health and blessings for the group and a closing prayer is said:

Beltane candles of love and light you shone forth your beauty and healed us this night. Thank you God and thank you Goddess for blessing us tonight and blessed be.

Everyone exits the circle chanting and drumming.

Solitary or Group Beltane Ritual

The world is within me

Prepare your Beltane altar with flowers, fertility goddess and the four elements with attention drawn towards the element of fire so lots of candles everywhere. Since Beltane is about fertility perhaps a picture of a soul mate or an object that represents the desire for love in your life such as a heart. A traditional emphasis has been around flowers and flowers can have spiritual meanings, so with that in mind go out to your local flower shop, or farmers market and select four flowers randomly or a mixed bouquet of flowers and bring them home. Now look up the spiritual meanings of the flowers that you have bought and incorporate that into your ritual.

Four candles pointing in the four directions east, south, west and north, surround a Beltane candle. These in turn are surrounded by thirteen stones that represent the moons of the year. The colors of the altar and candles should resonate with springtime colors such as light greens, yellows and pinks. Place your smudge bowl or cauldron to the side of your altar.

With your ceremonial feather, smudge the area, yourself and then offer smudge to the seven directions. Smudge upwards to the Creator, downward to Mother Earth and then the center of wheel itself. To the spiritual east, give thanks for the element of fire. To the emotional south, give thanks to the element of water. To the physical west, give thanks for the element of earth. To the north, which is mental, give thanks to the element of air.

Before I begin, I make this gesture and affirmation. I take my prayer stick in my left hand and draw the Celtic cross starting above my head I point my broom/wand upward and whisper *The Divine Creator*. I bring my prayer stick to the ground and say *Mother Earth*. I then go to the left of my body holding my stick I say *Sacred Door Keepers*. I bring my stick to the right of me and say *Sacred Earth Teachers*. Lastly, I make a circle and say *Sacred Circle of Life*. I lay my prayer stick down on a cloth and take another deep breath and stretch my arms out to form a cross. I say this prayer:

I stand, in the center of this sacred circle with arms outstretched in a pose of gratitude. I arise today through the power of the Creation that supports me, blesses me and heals me. I give thanks for my life and for nature and I humbly ask for Divine guidance in my life. May there be beauty above me, beauty within me and beauty below me.

When all is set up, light your candles. Say a prayer as you light your Beltane candle:

I light this candle to celebrate the light half of the year from Samhain eve to Beltane eve. I am grateful for my steady progress and tender blessings. This is the season for prosperity, fertility and peace for me and my loved ones.

Facing east light your eastern candle and acknowledge your flower Earth Teacher. In this direction if your flower is say tulip, give thanks for the wisdom that tulip has to offer you. Look up the magical properties of this flower. This is a message for you from the Creator. Do this in each direction with your four flowers. Over the course of spring keep those selected Earth Teachers in your home and be open to their wisdom, they are meant to be a blessing and a guide to you at this time.

Of course it wouldn't be Beltane without jumping the fire so place your candle on the floor and make a wish and jump over your candle and Happy Beltane!

Note: If you are doing this in a group it would be really special to know the number of people coming and everyone bring a flower along with its spiritual meanings written down and tied to the flower to give to someone else. After the ritual, offer your flower to the earth either by burning it, burying it, hanging it outside or offering it to water.

Finish by thanking the God and Goddess.

Thank you God and thank you Goddess for blessing us tonight and blessed be.

Everyone exits the circle chanting and drumming.

Summer Solstice Ritual

Love, light and spice

Summer Solstice or Litha in pagan circles is a beautiful time of year. The warmth of summer and the lusciousness of nature comforts us. If you have decided to have a summer solstice party this ritual is perfect it celebrates the longest day of the year with candlelight and encourages love in our lives with affirmations about soul mates and harmony in our families. This ceremony is simple yet meaningful and easy to put together. After the ceremony, you can have a feast, you can perform some divination for each other using fairy cards or whatever resonates with yourself. If you like you can use God and Goddess in your ritual or you can use Creator or even just Creation, the choice is yours depending on your spiritual path. Thank you for taking the journey with me Happy Summer Solstice.

Items you will need for this ceremony
Candles
Room to make a triangle of light
Essential oil and carrier oil
Bowls

Reflections before the ritual

Summer for most of us is our favorite time of year. Warm days followed by warm nights are perfect for enjoying nature and loved ones company. The fullness of life is all around us, the earth is lush and alive. Warm summer nights turn our thoughts to romance and love. Litha's warm breath is enchanting and she casts her spell over the hardest of hearts ... summer brings love.

This is the longest day of the year, the long lazy days of summer stretch before us, visions of vacations, beaches, hiking in woods keep our minds busy. Upon this summer's eve, we gather to honor Mother Earth and all her glory. This is the summer solstice the triumph of darkness, hand-to-hand we shall turn the wheel tonight for love and light. With the power of our hearts, we take responsibility for our choices and our fate; we chose our destinies. We are love, we walk in love we are surrounded by love we know the spice of life is love.

The purpose of the ceremony is to celebrate the gift of light, the power of our hearts to create our realities, the power of love. Mix some essential oils like lavender or Patchouli oil with a carrier oil like grape seed or olive oil and then anoint your solstice candle with this mixture. During the anointing of the candle, pray for love and health for all who participate in the ritual this night. Everyone will light their own solstice candle. There will be three candles on the floor for people to walk around and those candles should also be anointed. Each person will need to anoint themselves with their candles this is done at the main table. When it is time to do this, give each person their own small dish of oil mixed with the essential oil ask them to mix it with one finger. Ask them to think of the intention of love and healing in their lives and then have them rub their hands together and breath in the scent of the oil. This is done so we can align ourselves with the essential oil and bless the oil.

The area of the ceremony is blessed with prayers and smudging. The two altars at the sides of the entrance of the circle are set up and blessed.

Everyone is smudged before entering the circle. Once everyone is inside ceremonial area, there is an opening prayer and an invocation for protection for the circle.

God and Goddess banish fear and pain from this circle
Watch over us day and night, so mote it be.

Take your wand, prayer stick, broom and point it to the east and begin to turn clockwise and pray.

In the east, south, west and north
A perfect circle casts love and hope
A perfect circle casts out fear and pain
We gather here tonight to raise the vibration of positivity and power
Come all, you are invited to this sacred space.
We have come here to celebrate the Summer Solstice

Then everyone holds their broom or each other's hands and walks three times clockwise in a circle this signifies turning the yearly wheel.

Winter, spring, summer, fall
We turn the wheel for the benefit of all
Winter, spring, summer, fall
We turn the wheel for ceremony calls.

Or any chant like Mother Earth or Spiral Chant is fine.

Now stop while the Circle Keeper says a prayer:

We ask for the God and Goddess's blessings over this gathering

(Face east): *Great Spirit of Light place of the rising sun*
Let there be light on our paths, let our fire always burn brightly with
love and compassion. We thank you for the gift of fire.

(Face south): *Great Spirit of Love; fill our cups with your sacred*
waters. We thank you for water, it is the lifeblood of Mother Earth
and it sustains our lives and all life on this planet. We thank you for
the gift of water.

(Face west): *Great Spirit of Life; thank you for our bodies thank you*
for our paths, never let us forget our connection to Mother Earth
and our connection to spirit. Thank you for the gift of earth.

(Face north): *Thank you Great Spirit for the Creation of the*
universe and souls. Thank you for the air we breathe, thank you for
the winds of creation — the four winds from the four kingdoms.
Thank you for the messages they bring to us. We thank you for the
gift of air.

May the gifts of nature and blessings of the wise sustain us this
night and throughout our lives.

The Summer Solstice Candle is anointed and lit for the sun and
for love. This ceremony is all about light and love at summer
time. The circle Keeper performs a prayer and a blessing for the
group that each will have a safe and happy summer and that love
will bless their lives.

The Circle Keeper then calls each person up to the table and
shows them how to dip their fingers into the oil that anointed the
solstice candle and dab some on their collarbone, forehead and

wrists or wherever they feel comfortable putting some of the scented oil.

At the first anointed solstice candle, the participant takes some oil from their dish, dabs some oil on their forehead, and affirms:

My thoughts are aligned with love.

They move onto the second anointed candle, dab some oil on their throats, and affirm:

My speech is aligned with love.

They move onto the third candle, anoint some oil on their chest, and affirm:

My heart is aligned with love.

When all the participants have finished performing the triangle of light, they go to the Circle Keeper who hands them a candle. The participant anoints the candle, lights it from the solstice candle, and affirms:

This candle by its light I welcome love this Solstice night.

They leave their candles on the main table beside the main solstice candle.

After each person has done this act of lighting their candle, they are asked to be seated and then perhaps some chanting can be done. Everyone should be in a relaxed meditative state.

After this, the Circle Keeper bows to everyone and everyone bows to the Circle Keeper and to others and affirms:

May the Goddess and God within me, honor the Goddess and God within you.

The Circle Keeper does not blow out the candles but asks everyone to come up and use the candlesnuffer to keep the intentions within the candle. Then each person takes their candles home to be burned. When the candles has burned down any remaining bits should be buried into Mother Earth and given thanks for.

Everyone exits through the blessed gates.

Solitary or Group Summer Solstice Ritual

The world is within me

Prepare your summer altar with lots of greenery, flowers and grains for summer is the fullness of life. Have something on the altar to represent each of the elements. Then smudge the area and yourself and offer smudge smoke to the seven directions before the ritual.

You will need five candles. The center candle represents the God/Goddess, Creator or Creation. Four candles surround the inner candle. These outer candles will represent your Earth Teachers which reside in the southern quadrant of your Earth Wheel and which are the swimmers. The candle that is actually pointing south is the custodian of this southern quadrant; for me this is the Apple Tree. My three remaining candles /Earth Teachers for the southern quadrant are whale, dolphin and goldfish.

I next light my smudge within my bowl and offer smudge smoke to the seven directions.

Before I begin, I make this gesture and affirmation. I take my prayer stick in my left hand and draw the Celtic cross starting above my head I point my broom/wand upward and whisper *The Divine Creator.* I bring my prayer stick to the ground and say *Mother Earth.* I then go to the left of my body holding my stick I say *Sacred Door Keepers.* I bring my stick to the right of me and say *Sacred Earth Teachers.* Lastly, I make a circle and say *Sacred Circle of Life.* I lay my prayer stick down on a cloth and take another deep breath and stretch my arms out to form a cross. I say this prayer:

> *I stand, in the center of this sacred circle with arms outstretched in a pose of gratitude. I arise today through the power of the Creation that supports me, blesses me and heals me. I give thanks for my life and for nature and I humbly ask for Divine guidance in my life. May there be beauty above me, beauty within me and beauty below me.*

Facing south, light your Creator candle and give thanks for the four winds that bring us the seasons and the warm southern wind that brings us summer. Next light your custodian candle (for me this is the candle that represents the Apple Tree). I give thanks for this Earth Teacher and then I proceed to light all my Earth Teacher candles giving thanks for them as I light each candle. At the summer solstice, the earth is alive with growth and activity it is her busy time of year and so I take extra time to really feel and maintain my connection to the elements.

I allow the smoke to rise upwards and I give thanks for the water, which is the lifeblood of Mother Earth. I have a drink of grape juice or red wine and give thanks for the air that I breathe and the warm summer winds that will bring much joy in the coming season. I gaze at my candles and give thanks for the fire that I will enjoy as bonfires throughout the warm summer months. I touch all my flowers give thanks to earth whose beauty will be out in full force throughout the summer months giving us luscious fruits and vegetables to enjoy all season long. Lastly, I bring some smoke to my heart and acknowledge I have a deep connection to nature.

This is my emotional side of my Earth Wheel; the warmth of the summer sun reminds me of the warmth of love. I ask for the love of the Goddess/God, Creator to flow through all of the elements of this world and for that healing and loving energy to flow through each one of us. Holding each of my elements, I say a prayer over them asking the Great Mystery to heal all of the elements of this world and to balance all of the energies of this world.

I perform a blessing over an object that represents my lover or something that represents a potential lover. I take a rope of flowers or silk and I tie it around the object, which can be as simple as a crystal. I pray for love, peace, joy and harmony. I will be leaving this items on my altar for nine days, praying over them every day, then I will offer it to the earth (I bury it by a tree).

I finish my ritual with drumming and chanting.

Lammas Ritual

Lammas is the first of the harvests in pagan circles. If you have decided to have a Lammas party this ritual is perfect, it is simple yet meaningful and easy to put together. After the ceremony, you can have a feast; you can perform some divination for each other using runes, cards whatever resonates with yourself. If you like you can use God and Goddess in your ritual or you can use Creator or even just Creation, the choice is yours depending on your spiritual path. Thank you for taking the journey with me Happy Lammas.

Items you will need for this ceremony

Herbs to smudge with

Fruit, vegetables, meat or fish (or substitute), grains such as rice and beans

A Lammas loaf of bread

Tables (one center, one in each direction, and two at the entrance)

Six candles on center table and one each at the four directions.

Bowls

Reflections before the ritual

Lammas is the first of the harvest rituals, at this time the energies of Mother Earth are beginning to decline. We notice that the sun feels a bit weaker and they days are growing shorter. These are still the dog days of summer though and our last chance to enjoy the heat and warmth before our slide into autumn. It is a time to take stock of our lives and our talents. What have we sown this year and what are we reaping?

Driving in the countryside, we see the wheat fields, cornfields the earth is ripe and ready to give over her wealth to us. How perfect is this balance of giving and receiving. The farmers feed their soil and crops and Mother Earth in return feeds our bodies and keeps us alive. It is so important for us to have a healthy attitude about our food and to really appreciate where it comes from.

The purpose of this ritual is all about giving thanks, and sharing our foods with each other and asking ourselves what we have done to help others through the year. Perhaps donating or helping out at a food bank or if you are in need maybe it is time to seek out help and find out where there are resources that can offer you assistance. We all have times in our lives of plenty and being needful. There is no shame in being honest with ourselves.

In this ceremony, we will be offering food in each direction and after the ceremony use the foods from the ritual to have a feast and enjoy the bounty from Mother Earth.

The preparation for this ritual involves having blessed gates at the entry point of the circle, which is a small table that holds blessed candles, blessed statues of angels and deities, cleansed crystals whatever you chose to be a source of protection to keep unwanted negative energies out of your circle.

Your two altars that sit on either side of your circle and your center altar should all have a theme of harvest and warm tones of color.

The ceremony

The area of the ceremony is blessed with prayers and smudging. The two altars at the sides of the entrance of the circle are set up and blessed.

Everyone is smudged before entering the circle. Once everyone is inside ceremonial area, there is an opening prayer and an invocation for protection for the circle.

God and Goddess banish fear and pain from this circle
Watch over us day and night, so mote it be.

Take your wand, prayer stick, broom and point it to the east and begin to turn clockwise and pray.

In the east, south, west and north
A perfect circle casts love and hope
A perfect circle casts out fear and pain
We gather here tonight to raise the vibration of positivity and power
Come all, you are invited to this sacred space.
We have come here to celebrate Lammas

Then everyone holds their broom or each other's hands and walks three times clockwise in a circle this signifies turning the yearly wheel.

Winter, spring, summer, fall
We turn the wheel for the benefit of all
Winter, spring, summer, fall

We turn the wheel for ceremony calls.

Or any chant like Mother Earth or Spiral Chant is fine.

Now stop while the Circle Keeper says a prayer:

We ask for the God and Goddess's blessings over this gathering

(Face east): *Great Spirit of Light place of the rising sun Let there be light on our paths, let our fire always burn brightly with love and compassion. We thank you for the gift of fire.*

(Face south): *Great Spirit of Love; fill our cups with your sacred waters. We thank you for water, it is the lifeblood of Mother Earth and it sustains our lives and all life on this planet. We thank you for the gift of water.*

(Face west): *Great Spirit of Life; thank you for our bodies thank you for our paths, never let us forget our connection to Mother Earth and our connection to spirit. Thank you for the gift of earth.*

(Face north): *Thank you Great Spirit for the Creation of the universe and souls. Thank you for the air we breathe, thank you for the winds of creation — the four winds from the four kingdoms. Thank you for the messages they bring to us. We thank you for the gift of air.*

May the gifts of nature and blessings of the wise sustain us this night and throughout our lives.

For the opening invocation, the Circle Keeper says:

I honor and greet you all, welcome to our circle.

Everyone sits.

Light the first candle for Lammas:

Lammas candle of love and light bless this sacred circle tonight

Light the second candle for peace.
Light the third candle for love.
Light the fourth candle for compassion.
Finally, light the fifth candle for hope.

The Circle Keeper prays:

This is Lammas our midsummer; the fields are filled with our natural foods that nourish our bodies, minds and our spirits. As the wheel of the year turns, we are in a cycle of blessing and abundance. Lammas the first festival of the harvest, we give thanks for the harvests in our lives both the divine and the mundane.

The host breaks a Lammas loaf into four quarters and hands pieces out to people in the group to take to the four tables situated at the four quarters of the circle. Then the host prays this prayer for protection of the circle and all who are within it.

We offer these Lammas loaves and ask that the light and love of the Creator sustain us, surround us and protect us.

We sing, chant and drum. We turn the wheel by dancing around the circle. We hold brooms, cords or each other's hands.

The Circle Keeper calls someone in the circle to come forward hands this person a bell and one of the lit candles and asks them to carry it to the east. The person rings the bell in the eastern quadrant of the circle and lights a candle that is situated on the small table and returns to their place in the circle and sits down.

The Circle Keeper calls another person to come forward,

hands them a bowl of fruit and sends them to the eastern table to place the food there. Everyone prays:

Thank you Mother Earth for our food, we pray for those who don't have enough food may you send us out to help those in need. Help us to eat foods that will nourish our spirits.

The Circle Keeper calls for another person to come forward and gives the bell and a lit candle and take it to the small southern table. The person will ring a bell and light the east candle and returns to their spot in the circle.

The Circle Keeper calls another to take a bowl of vegetables to the southern table:

We thank you Mother Earth for this food may all have enough to eat, help us to have a good emotional relationship with our food.

Again the Circle Keeper calls someone to come forth and is given the bell and lit candle. They go to the western table and light the candle and ring the bell and returns to their place.

The Circle Keeper calls someone to take a bowl of different kinds of rice and beans to the western part of the circle:

We give thanks for the healing power of foods over our physical ailments we thank them for healing cancer, heart disease and all diseases. We honor their ability to bring health to our bodies and to give us life.

One more time, the Circle Keeper calls someone to come forth, light a candle on the northern table, and ring the bell and return to their place.

The Circle Keeper calls someone to take the bowl of meats or cans of fish (or substitute) to the northern section of our circle:

We give thanks for our foods and ask that the foods that we eat will help us to have healthy minds.

When the circle has been completed the Circle Keeper calls for everyone to turn the wheel. Chanting and drumming is done three times to achieve harmony.

The host lights a candle for the harvest and walks the circle singing the Mother Earth Chant.

Everyone offers an herb to the smudge bowl or cauldron. This is done as an offering of thanks for the abundance in our lives or requesting abundance in our lives.

Closing prayer:

Here we are at Lammas it is midsummer, plants are still growing and sun is still warm. We are reminded to be grateful and to not be afraid to ask for help. Lammas is the first of the harvest celebrations and the first for winter preparations. Let us be wise as the farmer let us know when to gather and when to save. Let us give thanks for all we get whether it be modest or abundant. The cycle of blessings is our heritage it is our gift from the Creator and Mother Earth.

Now everyone stands and turns the wheel again with songs and chanting.

Everyone stops.

The Circle Keeper bows to everyone and everyone bows back and then to each other and affirms:

May the Goddess and God within me, honor the Goddess and God within you.

Everyone exits through the blessed gates.

Solitary or Group Lammas Ritual

Prepare your Lammas altar with items of the harvest. This is the first festival of the autumn festivals, it is the dark time of the year and it is a fire ceremony. Lammas is also about farewells and regrets.

Suggestions for the altar are breads, grains, preserves, herbs, herbal teas, honey, mead, a Lammas candle, moonstones, mini candles, and cauldron or smudge bowl. Use smudging herbs such as sweet grass and the altar cloth should be a dark color like black to signify that we are entering into the dark time of the year. Lammas is about harvest so make a wreath out of herbs and grains to decorate your home and altar area. Buy local preserves and enjoy them with your Lammas breads.

As you light your Lammas candle, take a moment to meditate on your regrets. What didn't you complete this summer? Lammas is also about farewells, so think of what or who is passing from your life.

The center two candles are for Lammas, one for farewells and regrets the other is for healing. Four mini candles surround these candles pointing to the four cardinal directions east, south, west and north. These candles can be of your own sacred colors. Surround them all with thirteen grandmother moon candles.

Smudge your area, self, and others and then offer smudge smoke to the seven directions

I make this gesture and affirmation. I take my prayer stick in my left hand and draw the Celtic cross starting above my head I point my broom/wand upward and whisper *The Divine Creator.* I bring my prayer stick to the ground and say *Mother Earth.* I then go to the left of my body holding my stick I say *Sacred Door Keepers.* I bring my stick to the right of me and say *Sacred Earth*

Teachers. Lastly, I make a circle and say *Sacred Circle of Life*. I lay my prayer stick down on a cloth and take another deep breath and stretch my arms out to form a cross. I say this prayer:

> *I stand, in the center of this sacred circle with arms outstretched in a pose of gratitude. I arise today through the power of the Creation that supports me, blesses me and heals me. I give thanks for my life and for nature and I humbly ask for Divine guidance in my life. May there be beauty above me, beauty within me and beauty below me.*

Once everything is ready, light all your candles except the two Lammas candles. Have your smudge bowl or cauldron placed to the side of your altar. Place your bread covered with preserves and/or honey somewhere on your altar with a clean linen cloth over it.

Now think of your regrets and farewells and light your first Lammas candle. The color I like for this is brown. Think of healing and light. I prefer yellow for my second candle.

Now I turn and face the south (south is summer time in the wheel). I offer my herb to the smudge bowl, give thanks and affirm that I will nurture my emotional self and the emotional needs of my loved ones. I will not repress my emotions but deal with them in a grounded and reasonable way, which is healthy for my family and me. I give thanks for the element of water, which is the lifeblood of Mother Earth and all her creatures including me. I take a drink of water from my chalice.

I then turn to the west I offer my herb to the fire and give thanks for the foods and herbs that nourish my body and give thanks for the element of earth. I eat some bread.

Turning to the north, I offer my herb to the smudge bowl and give thanks for my mental health and promise to nurture all that is positive and good within me. It is important to bring forth a harvest of kind words for others so I place paper with positive words written on them and burn them. I give thanks to the element of air. I appreciate the fresh air that I breathe and promise to take care of my lungs and to take time for a deep cleansing breath each day then I take some deep cleansing breaths.

I finish facing east I offer my herb to the smudge bowl and give thanks for the element of fire. Fire warms our homes, burns our sacred items and keeps friends close. I promise to keep my spiritual treasures where they are safe and to see the spiritual in all things.

Take your bread and tea or mead and give a prayer of thanks over it. Sprinkle the bread with herbs such as rosemary, offer some to the earth, and then enjoy some yourself before passing it around if there are others joining you in the ritual. Enjoy some bread with preserves or honey and the herbal tea or mead.

Follow this with chanting and drumming.

If you've made a Lammas wreath smudge it now and it is ready to be hung on your wall or near your altar area.

Closing prayer:

> *Lammas time comes, it is harvest time, Creator, God/Goddess bless us all, and blessed be.*

Autumn Equinox/Mabon Ritual

Autumn equinox is a special time of year. If you have decided to have an equinox party this ritual is perfect, it is simple yet meaningful and easy to put together. After the ceremony, you can have a feast; you can perform some divination for each other using runes, cards whatever resonates with yourself. If you wish, you can use God and Goddess in your ritual or you can use

Creator, or even just Creation, the choice is yours depending on your spiritual path. Thank you for taking the journey with me, Happy Mabon.

Items you will need for this ceremony
Bucket
Sand or dirt
Candles
Matches
Items that represent the elements
Herbs to smudge with such as sage or rosemary
Tables
Brooms or cords that people can hang onto when turning the wheel

Reflections before the ritual
Mabon is the autumn equinox a time when the day light is leaving us. The rosy warmth of summer is gone. The days are growing chilly and we certainly feel summer is visiting at some other sunny shore. The harvest moon is rounding in the evening sky. Canadian geese can be heard flying by heading south. Watching the geese flying formation makes me feel like a child being left behind. Red leaves bleed down upon Mother Earth in a flood of color. The scent of autumn is heavy in the air. Everywhere we see nature preparing for winter and as I watch the changes, I realize that the wheel of the year keeps turning.

Autumn rituals are about closures and endings we banish what is bane and what no longer serves us. Mabon brings times of transformations, as the earth winds down and the harvest is being gathered, it is time for us to reflect, and scrutinize our own harvests. Let us reflect on memories that we want to hang onto and regrets we need to let go of.

Crispy mornings, bright blue skies, apple stands by the roadside filled with the bounty of the orchard, all make me want to reflect on what bounties that I need to be grateful for. Walking on brisk autumn evenings, I sense the winds are whispering to me that the spirits are near and the veil is growing thinner as the wheel is turning towards Samhain. The aging sun can rule us no longer let us dance and make magick in the moonlight.

Come gather with us in this sacred place. Join us now for as in the ways of old, our power freely flows as our power grows.

The purpose of the ceremony is to sort out in our minds what memories we'd like to hang onto and to allow ourselves to let regrets and pain wither and die. The candles that we light are the memories and gifts that we want to hang onto that for which we want to give thanks. The candles we blow out represent pain and regret. Therefore, when we blow out our candles we are saying goodbye to our regrets.

On your tables you can have a small bucket with sand in it filled with pillar candles, or you can have mini candles on a table, the choice is yours, but make sure you have matches on the table or one lit candle that people can use to light their own candle from.

In your bucket of sand or dirt, you can have candles for each person or a small table with a mini candle for each person.

The Circle Keeper will stand at the center of the circle and there should be a table decorated for autumn. Have two pillar candles one should be a lighter color like yellow or white and one should be a darker color like brown or black. These colors represent the perfect balance of light and dark that happens on the equinox. How we need to seek balance in our lives.

The Circle Keeper will want a steady flow of people walking around the tables with the candles on them. Some people will be lighting their candles and then moving onto blowing some candles out.

After the chanting and prayers the Circle Keeper will turn to the first person and call them forth to light a candle for what they have to be thankful for, then he will ask another and another.

After the person has lit their candle the Circle Keeper will tell them to go to the next table and think of regrets and unpleasant memories that need to be let go and then that person will meditate a moment then blow out their candle.

The ceremony

The area of the ceremony is blessed with prayers and smudging. The two altars at the sides of the entrance of the circle are set up and blessed.

Everyone is smudged before entering the circle. Once everyone is inside ceremonial area, there is an opening prayer and an invocation for protection for the circle.

God and Goddess banish fear and pain from this circle
Watch over us day and night, so mote it be.

Take your wand, prayer stick, broom and point it to the east and begin to turn clockwise and pray.

In the east, south, west and north
A perfect circle casts love and hope
A perfect circle casts out fear and pain
We gather here tonight to raise the vibration of positivity and power
Come all, you are invited to this sacred space.
We have come here to celebrate Lammas

Then everyone holds their broom or each other's hands and walks three times clockwise in a circle this signifies turning the yearly wheel.

Winter, spring, summer, fall
We turn the wheel for the benefit of all
Winter, spring, summer, fall

We turn the wheel for ceremony calls.

Or any chant like Mother Earth or Spiral Chant is fine.

Now stop while the Circle Keeper says a prayer:

We ask for the God and Goddess's blessings over this gathering

(Face east): *Great Spirit of Light place of the rising sun Let there be light on our paths, let our fire always burn brightly with love and compassion. We thank you for the gift of fire.*

(Face south): *Great Spirit of Love; fill our cups with your sacred waters. We thank you for water, it is the lifeblood of Mother Earth and it sustains our lives and all life on this planet. We thank you for the gift of water.*

(Face west): *Great Spirit of Life; thank you for our bodies thank you for our paths, never let us forget our connection to Mother Earth and our connection to spirit. Thank you for the gift of earth.*

(Face north): *Thank you Great Spirit for the Creation of the universe and souls. Thank you for the air we breathe, thank you for the winds of creation — the four winds from the four kingdoms. Thank you for the messages they bring to us. We thank you for the gift of air.*

May the gifts of nature and blessings of the wise sustain us this night and throughout our lives.

The Circle Keeper says:

I honor and greet you all, welcome to our circle.
Moon of the night and sun of the day the eternal balance of light and

dark; here we seek our eternal balance on this Mabon night.

The Circle Keeper lights one of the two pillar candles at center table (white candle or yellow candle).

We light this candle for our harvest of memories, what we have, our own storehouse of self-strengths and gifts. In nature, we see again the balance of giving and receiving. This is a witch's thanksgiving. As the year continues to wane, we have a sense of endings, this is a good time to let go of regrets and painful memories. Just as the trees let go of their dead leaves, we let go of our pain. Now we light the darker candle for letting go of regrets in order that we can attain balance in our lives.

The Circle Keeper will call people forward to light their candles for giving thanks and proceeding to the tables of lit candles and blowing them out to signify letting go of regrets.

Now the group can do some chanting and drumming.

The Circle Keeper performs a blessing on the group. He or she will ask people to come forward to help. One person will walk around and sprinkle some corn meal, another with water, another will touch each person lightly with a feather and another or the Circle Keeper will walk holding a candle.

An invocation will be something like this:

Air I request of thee to gift us with intellect and creativity.
Fire I request of thee to fill us with purpose and passion.
Earth I request of thee to keep us balanced and focused.
Water I request of thee to help us be intuitive and receptive.

Now everyone stands and turns the wheel again with songs and chanting.

Everyone stops and the Circle Keeper bows to everyone and everyone bows to the Circle Keeper and to each other and affirms:

> *May the Goddess and God within me, honor the Goddess and God within you.*

Everyone exits through the blessed gates.

Solitary or Group Autumn Equinox Ritual

The altar set up with much in the way of red, gold, wheat, apples, pinecones, nuts and all items that pertain to harvest and autumn. You will need smudging materials, shakers, bell for ringing and cards for divination. If possible make a wheat braid for each person.

Smudge area yourself and smudge to the seven directions.

I make this gesture and affirmation. I take my prayer stick in my left hand and draw the Celtic cross starting above my head I point my broom/wand upward and whisper *The Divine Creator*. I bring my prayer stick to the ground and say *Mother Earth*. I then go to the left of my body holding my stick I say *Sacred Door Keepers*. I bring my stick to the right of me and say *Sacred Earth Teachers*. Lastly, I make a circle and say *Sacred Circle of Life*. I lay my prayer stick down on a cloth and take another deep breath and stretch my arms out to form a cross. I say this prayer:

> *I stand, in the center of this sacred circle with arms outstretched in a pose of gratitude. I arise today through the power of the Creation that supports me, blesses me and heals me. I give thanks for my life and for nature and I humbly ask for Divine guidance in my life. May there be beauty above me, beauty within me and beauty below me.*

Prayer for protection and blessing during the ceremony:

The leaves begin to turn from green to brilliant reds and yellows, animals start to migrate, and the harvest is underway This is the autumn equinox a equal time of day and night and so we celebrate the balance of Mabon. Creator of the Universe we are travelling now into our dark mother time. The days grow shorter, the nights grow longer, and so we gather here tonight to celebrate our trip into the dark half of the year. This is harvest time and a time to reflect of how fortunate we are and how blessed we are. For all our moments of pain let there be love, for our moments of illness let there be healing, for all moments of despair let there be hope, for our moments of fear let there be strength and protection.

If you are in a group have everyone sit around the center altar or fire.

The Circle Keeper hands out papers with this prayer written down on it and everyone recites:

As the wheel of the year continues to turn, each season passes onto the next. This is the natural flow of our world. Guide us Creator in your wisdom. Show us what was, what will be, and what is to come.

This is a time for selecting of cards for a message. Pass a card deck around and let everyone pick a card or select a card for you. Alternatively, have them come up to the altar pick one read it and place it back in the deck. Perform this part of the ritual in the manner that bests works for you

After everyone has their message you can proceed to the next level of ceremony. Perform some chanting, drumming so that everyone can relax and absorb the messages they have received.

The Circle Keeper stands and prays over the group:

The Equinox is upon us, and the time to reflect, at hand. All time comes together, here and now in this sacred space. We feel the changes in nature and within us. We are all connected, the Creator will heal and restore nature and us too, back to perfect balance as long as we listen and follow the natural rhythms in nature. Healers come forward...

Anyone who feels led to pray over people can do so now, this is the healing portion of the ritual.

Everyone now stands, stretch their legs and joins hands. They should all move around sunwise or clockwise in a circle. Take this moment to reflect on the beauty of nature and the autumn time that is now at hand.

Now there should be chanting and singing.

The Earth Teacher of wheat gives us abundance, and financial blessings but we should not focus too much on money. We do need it to take care of our loved one and animals and to support the charities we feel so passionately about. We should be grateful for prosperity and pray for it. I like to make a decoration with wheat and place a coin in it. This act reminds me to touch it and pray for my finances while affirming that all my financial needs are taken care of.

Each person can be given a small wheat braid and then pray:

We raise our wheat and give thanks. We ask for blessings for ourselves, our loved ones. We ask for blessings to circle our world that the suffering will be stopped and the hungry will be fed. We affirm that we are blessed, we are prosperous, we are healed, and all our needs are met. We offer our wheat to the fire or altar

The wheat braids should be later offered to the earth either by burying it, burning it, throwing it in the water or the earth either by burying it, burning it, throwing it in the water or hanging it in a tree.

Everyone sits down and the Circle Keeper starts with her/his offering then directs others to share and discuss their harvest offering and what it means to them.

Select four items from the earth that represents the harvest and before the ceremony look up the mystical properties of this item and share that with the group, it will mean something to you or someone else.

Chant:

> *In Life is Death, and in Death is Life.*
> *The Sacred Dance goes on and on*
> *From whence we came, we shall return*
> *And come again.*
> *Seasons pass, and pass again,*
> *The circle stays unbroken*

Offer your wreath to the fire or cauldron. Remember to make your offering as beautiful as possible. This is the season of death, dying and decay; it is a natural part of a natural process of our world.

Chant:

> *Sacred knowledge is within us all*
> *Our Ancestors have all sat in circles*
> *And have prayed for us to find our paths*

Appendices

Earth Teachers: Herbs, Oils and Crystals within the Earth Wheel

In the Earth Wheel, you have herbs to smudge with and herbs that can be Earth Teachers. Crystals can also be Earth Teachers. These are a few herbs that I use particularly for smudging I hope you try them but there are many more, make sure you do your research before you use an herb to make sure it isn't toxic.

Sweet grass it has a fruity and floral scent that attracts positive energies.

Mugwort it has an earthy scent and is very grounding there is something mysterious and ancient about this herb that is intriguing

Sage has various scents depending on the type. I happen to love desert sage, this herbs repels negative entities.

Lavender scent is very uplifting and is excellent at attracting positive energies such as angels.

Cedar is very good at clearing spaces from negative energies and so is frankincense. **Tobacco** is a powerful cleansing herb it will rid the environment of negativity. Sweet pine is grounding. It has a soft aroma and will settle the space down and make it ready for ritual.

Within my wheel, I have trees at each of my cardinal points, but the wheel is personal and so you can use whatever you feel led to use, such as herbs, flowers and crystals.

The beings that stand at the cardinal points also known as Door Keepers or custodians are guards that protect an area, so with that in mind I always select something that has a protective feel about it.

I think all trees have a protective quality about them, so I will not suggest any, just choose a tree you love and feel a connection with.

If you are going to use herbs in your wheel for custodians, select the ones that have protective medicinal qualities such as slippery elm or chamomile.

Crystals can be custodians and so same thing applies here to, select crystals that have a protective aura about them such as onyx.

An Earth Wheel is a personal thing, so select items from nature that you love make this ceremony your own, I hope this brings you closer to nature and helps you to become aware that we are part of this marvelous ecosystem.

I will make a list of some herbs and crystals that I am attracted to that I believe have a protective personality.

Below is a list of just a few herbs and crystals that you might want to consider using in your ceremony.

Earth Teacher Herbs

Catnip: Wards off evil, money, happiness

Cedar: Protection, thoughtfulness, marriage and partnerships

Echinacea: Strength, courage, uplifting, encouragement

Eucalyptus: Protection, clears blockages, gives direction

Lavender: Sweet gatherings, bliss, friendship, purification

Lemon Balm: Graciousness, soothing to nerves, fights stress

Mugwort: Caution, fertility, wisdom, connection with ancestors

Passion Flower: Love, passion, friendship, protection

Peppermint: Purifies, mental power, wisdom sensibility

Tobacco: Healing, invocation, connection with spirit, protection

Rose: Love, divine communication, loyalty, strength

Rosemary: Protection, wards off evil, stops gossip, attracts friendly visitors to your home

Sage: Purification, dispels negativity, promotes peace and balance

Sweet grass: healing, strength, perseverance, abundance, calling

spirits of the light, attracts angels
Sweet Pine: Luck, money, success, opportunities
Thyme: Health, sleep, dream recall, courage, strength
Violet: Modesty, virtue, watchfulness, faithfulness
Yarrow: Courage, exorcism, protection, purification

Earth Teacher Essential Oils

Basil: Defends against fatigue, burnout, exhaustion, memory
Bergamot: Defends against anger, anxiety, depression, stress
Cinnamon: Concentration, mental fatigue, connection to spirit
Clary Sage: Fear, panic attacks, grounding
Frankincense: Grief, peace, happiness, prayers to heaven
Jasmine: Confidence, joy, protects against negative energies
Lavender: Strength, panic attacks, peace, love, joy
Roman Chamomile: Stops anger, irritability
Rose: Love, promotes peacefulness, sleep, wards off panic
Rosewood: Emotional imbalances, stress, very calming
Ylang Ylang: Helps with PMS, mood swings, fear

Earth Teacher Resins

Copal: Protection, clearing negativity and fearfulness
Dragons blood: Love, protection, exorcism
Frankincense: psychic visions, protection, exorcism, spirituality
Myrrh: Prayers, perfection, love, psychic visions
Sandalwood: Protection, clearing, balancing, grounding

Earth Teacher Woods

Apple: Cycle of birth, death and rebirth, healing, abundance
Birch: Purification, connection to ancestors, safe travel
Cherry: Passion, love, will, desire
Cinnamon: Protection, sweetness of life, joy, heals grief
Hazel: Wisdom, stability, beauty, love, creativity
Lilac: Expansion, growth, spiritual happiness
Maple: Steadfastness, strength, family ties, sweetness of life

Pine: Shields against troubles, comforts sorrowfulness, ancestors

Rowan (Mountain Ash): Bestowing happiness, enhances relationships, wards off negative people and situations, peace

Sandalwood: Truth, wisdom, family ties, memories, prosperity

Earth Teacher Crystals

Agate: A protector of children, prosperity, endows a person with patience

Amazonite: Good stone for business or looking for employment, calming and soothing, increases self-respect

Amber: Protects aura from unhealthy energies, brings luck and happiness, grounding

Amethyst: Grounding promotes stability, quiets the mind, promotes restful sleep

Angelite: Balancing, aligning the physical body with the aura, attracts angels

Bloodstone: Alleviates pain, cleanses blood, gives courage and strength

Botswana: Beneficial for circulatory system, warms cold limbs, balances emotions

Calcite: Mental alertness, good for people who are healers, helps dream recall

Carnelian: Gives confidence, boldness, helps people to take the initiative, and stimulates appetite

Citrine: Good for emotional and mental clarity

Dioptase: Heals the heart, releases sadness and pain, heals past life hurts, heals memories, good for heart and lungs

Emerald: Love, fortune, money stone, abundance, opens doors for opportunities and growth, expansion

Fluorite: Teeth, bones, detoxes the body, mood stabilizer, helps fight anxiety

Garnet: Brings love into our lives, keeps love in our lives, stimulates faith, helps visions from the divine

Gold: Prosperity, healing, love, helps digestion, connection to the divine

Hematite: Grounding, helps in exams, restores equilibrium, astral protection

Herkimer Diamond: Use with meditation, assist in finding life path, healing, remember past lives

Jade: Wealth, health, happiness, joy, stamina, balancing, healing

Jet: Protection, connection to ancestors, memories of past lives, healing past lives, grounding

Kunzite: Creates loving thoughts, uplifting, compassion, centering

Labradorite: Creativity, will power, healers stone, attracts friendships and restores old friendships

Lapis Lazuli: Quiets the mind, prosperity, helps hearing, money stone, promotes self acceptance

Moonstone: Helps women, helps men be in touch with their feminine side, connection with ancestors, heals memories, helps with psychic power

Obsidian: Grounding, helps people see unhealthy patterns in their lives, promotes self-esteem

Onyx: Balances, grounds, protection, good for heart

Peridot: Wealth, protection, good for throat area, good for stomach

Petrified Wood: Grounding, past life memories, direction, strength, helps us to defend ourselves

Rhondochrosite: Soul mates, twin flames, karma, past lives, love, heals relationships

Sapphire: Protection, safe passage on water, traveler's stone, antidepressant

Selenite: Represses anger, record Keeper, Ascended Masters, happiness, angels, guides

Sodalite: Intuition, balances brain, balances hormones, helps mood swings, money stone

Sunstone: Warms the heart, happiness, helps blood circulation, repels possessive people, promotes clarity

Tiger Eye: Money stone, helps in exams, helps in legal issues, grounding, helps nerves

Tourmaline: Protection from psychic attack, helps in decision making, connection to your guides

Turquoise: Connections to the Creator, truth, protection, money, success, strength from ancestors

Zorsite: Helps joint pain, heals heart from hurt, promotes trust in the divine, tonic for body

Spiritual Properties of Colors

Red: Love, lust, courage, strength

Orange: Independence, happiness, vigor

Yellow: Intelligence, clarity, mental power

Green: Healing, grounding, logical

Blue: Peace, spirituality, health

Purple: Spiritual energy, psychic power, healing

White: Protection, peace, spirituality, strength

Black: Absorption of negative energies, sacrifice

Pink: Love, harmony, calming

Gold: Masculine energy, prosperity, spiritual shield

Silver: Feminine energy, spiritual shield, creative

Lavender: Intuition, self-love, tranquility

Thirteen Moons of Creation

January Moon — Cedar: The cedar is an evergreen. These are grandmothers of the earth. During cedar moon remember your grandmother's advice, keep your feet dry, and keep your chest warm. This month it is all about being sensible and practical. Offer cedar during full moon.

February Moon — Bannock Moon: This bread was important to the Métis people and first nation's people. Giver of life, bread of survival in tough times, you should know who is friend and foe. Travel the safe road and known road. During these tough months of winter it isn't wise to travel in unknown areas, this lesson teaches us to wait, learn and research before decisions.

Bake some bannock and offer it to Mother Earth during full moon.

March Moon — Maple Moon: The sweet sap of the forest, winds of change are approaching, getting ready to unleash restraints from winter and enjoy nature. Maple teaches us to look after our bodies, especially our blood, this sap is the blood of the maple tree and so we are reminded to take care of our diets, our hearts.

Offer some maple to the earth during this full moon for healing of your heart and blood.

April Moon — Dandelion Moon: Spring has come and with it the flowers of the earth. Dandelion is such an important herb for health. There are numerous benefits to drinking the leaf from this plant. Be mindful of this herb and do not treat it with disrespect spraying the ground with harmful poisons. Be mindful of polluting our planet say sorry and promise to make better decisions around all you do.

Drink some dandelion tea or offer the flower to the earth

during full moon.

May Moon —Chamomile Moon: Friendly, relaxing, and calming chamomile is a beautiful herb to drink and take when stressed. This herb is offered during May to help me to give thanks for the warmth that is here, finally no more snow, I feel happier and this herb resonates with this happiness.

I offer this herb now to ask for happiness in the coming months.

June Moon — Strawberry Moon: Strawberry time, the first fruits here in Canada that we all welcome and enjoy. It is so much fun to get out in strawberry fields and pick berries. Strawberry's red color reminds me to be careful about wearing my heart on my sleeve. There are people who can abuse sensitive people, do not cut yourself off but be careful who you open your heart to.

I offer strawberries this time of year and ask for soul mates to come into my life.

July Moon — Nutmeg Moon: Warm, sensuous nutmeg is a very earthy and grounding spice. It is good for aches and pains in our bodies. It also strengthens the connection to the divine. Under a nutmeg moon, you will feel more spiritual and earthy at the same time. Your head in the clouds but your feet firmly planted on the ground.

Make offerings for spiritual growth during this moon phase and for pain to be released.

August Moon —Sunflower Moon: Happy sunflowers they are so joyous to look at, they turn towards the sun. We need to make sure we are attuned to the natural rhythms in nature to. Early to bed and early to rise makes us healthy and wise. Make sure you are using wisdom in the sun balance the sunscreen times so you won't get sun damage. Remember though we do need a bit of sun to get our vitamin D just be sensible and have balance.

The sun reminds us of God the Father offer some sun flowers around your area of moon time celebration and reflect on the beauty of male and female, the yin and the yang of creation.

September Moon — Corn Moon: This plant is very important to people all over the world. This plant knows it is food and knows its purpose is to help other people and animals lives. This plant understands sacrifice and wishes to teach us how to make good sacrifices in our lives. We don't wish to be martyrs and make our lives miserable but there are always sacrifices that we must make, let us learn from corn to make wise ones.

Offer corn during this moon time for wisdom about this issue.

October Moon — Pumpkin Moon: It is autumn and with Thanksgiving, Halloween and Samhain our thoughts turn to festivals and holidays. This plant plays a major role in our lives during this time. The pumpkin has many benefits such as protection from certain cancers. It is rich in beta-carotene and potassium; it is anti-inflammatory so it is good for those aches and pains. Men should eat pumpkin seed weekly to protect their prostates. The spiritual side to this plant comes in ways of being nurturing and mothering to our souls offer this up for Mother Earth to send you people who will be kind and loving towards you.

November Moon — Cinnamon Moon: This fragrant spice is very healing to our bodies. Not only does it taste good but also it is very good for us, helps our blood, and is excellent for those with stomach or bone cancers. Spirituality it is very masculine and direct, it would work well with prayers to fight evil energies.

You could spread some cinnamon around your circle asking the spice to pray for you and to protect your home and space. Offer it during full moon for psychic protection

December Moon: Pine Moon, this evergreen is a natural source of vitamin C for the natives of North America. The Celts believed it to be a sacred tree along with indigenous people here in America. Old folks talk about stuffing it in beds to keep lice away. Burning it clears the air of sickness this tree desires to protect. People have close connections to it especially for holidays.

The tree is very cleansing and so offer some pine to the earth or burn some to clear negative energy and thoughts out of your aura and space.

The meanings of my moons each year do change. Each month I try to reflect on the meanings of the moon and mix it with ceremony.

Blue Moon: Great Spirit Moon, bringing together the powerful medicines of tobacco, cedar, sage and sweet grass. The Creator allows us moments to purify and renew. First, we cleanse than we renew. Under Grandmother Moon, we regain our strength and celebrate our spirituality, but we still remember those that suffer. We pray at the full moon time to be fortified so that when we return to present life we are stronger and healthier. The sacred medicines of tobacco, sage, sweet grass and cedar help us to know who we are and what we need to do. We have a common destiny to the earth when the herbs are healthy we are healthy so this is a time to connect to these sacred beings and work with them to heal the planet. Smudging and dancing during this moon to heal the earth.

Chants

Mother Earth Chant

The heartbeat of our mother is changing us
The heartbeat of our mother is reshaping us
The heartbeat of our mother is restoring us
We are her children she is our mother
We will honor her we will take care of her.

Earth is Our Mother Chant

The Earth is our mother, we must take care of her (x2)

Chorus: Hey yana, ho yana, hey yan yan,
Hey yana, ho yana, hey yan yan.

Her sacred ground we walk upon, with every step we take (x2)
The Earth is our mother, she will take care of us (x2)

Origin unknown. Recorded on: "The Circle Is Cast," Libana, 1986
"Songs of the Sacred Wheel, "Earth Dance Singers"

Spiral Chant

The earth, the air, the fire, the water
Return, return, return, return

Cherokee Morning Chant

We n' de ya ho, We n' de ya ho,
We n' de ya, We n' de ya Ho ho ho ho,
He ya ho, He ya ho, Ya ya ya

Afterword

What is an earth based spiritual path mean? My ancestors will say it is honoring all your relatives; the rocks, the plants, the four legged, two legged, creepers and crawlers, swimmers and the winged ones. The ancient ones taught us that all life is sacred and all forms of life have spiritual significance to each other and to us. Our higher-evolved relatives understand this though many humans do not. I believe that to follow an earth based spiritual path means to have a desire to live in harmony and respect with nature. The smudging and the rituals are all reflections and demonstrations of your acknowledgement that you are linked to all the Earth Teachers of the planet and that you are open and willing to learn from them the mysteries of life.

Grandmother Cedar whispers: *life is beauty and promise blended together. A butterfly will fly by and send you the gift of pure joy.* Yet this path can mean more. Perhaps it is when lying within the womb of your mother; with a cry, you take her essence into your lungs. She is your lifeblood; she is the flesh on your bones. The day you were formed Mother Earth's wisdom melded your spirit and when you were born, she announced your birth to the four winds of creation.

Mother Earth sees her child and she smiles.

MOON
BOOKS

Moon Books invites you to begin or deepen your encounter with Paganism, in all its rich, creative, flourishing forms.